DOCUMENTING
IMPOSSIBLE REALITIES

DOCUMENTING IMPOSSIBLE REALITIES

Ethnography, Memory, and the As If

**Susan Bibler Coutin and
Barbara Yngvesson**

CORNELL UNIVERSITY PRESS   ITHACA AND LONDON

First published 2023 by Cornell University Press

Library of Congress Cataloging-in-Publication Data

Names: Coutin, Susan Bibler, author. | Yngvesson, Barbara, 1941– author.
Title: Documenting impossible realities : ethnography, memory, and the as if / Susan Bibler Coutin and Barbara Yngvesson.
Description: Ithaca [New York] : Cornell University Press, 2023. | Includes bibliographical references and index.
Identifiers: LCCN 2022023470 (print) | LCCN 2022023471 (ebook) | ISBN 9781501768828 (hardcover) | ISBN 9781501768880 (paperback) | ISBN 9781501768866 (pdf) | ISBN 9781501768873 (epub)
Subjects: LCSH: Belonging (Social psychology) | Identity (Psychology)— Social aspects. | Marginality, Social. | Social integration. | Mind and reality—Social aspects. | Ethnology.
Classification: LCC HM753 .C688 2023 (print) | LCC HM753 (ebook) | DDC 302.5—dc23/eng/20221024
LC record available at https://lccn.loc.gov/2022023470
LC ebook record available at https://lccn.loc.gov/2022023471

To Sigfrid and Curt

Contents

Acknowledgments

We are grateful to the National Science Foundation Law and Social Sciences Program, which funded both Susan Coutin's research (grant numbers SES-1061063 and SES-1535501) and Barbara Yngvesson's research (grant numbers SES-9113894 and SBR-9511937). Any opinions, findings, and conclusions or recommendations expressed in this material are those of the authors and do not necessarily reflect the views of the National Science Foundation. The University of California Humanities Research Institute hosted us for a Collaborative Research Residency during a critical period of our research and writing. Visits to the International Institute for the Sociology of Law (IISL) were also productive for our thinking, and we are grateful for IISL's support. The University of Southern California Center for Law, History and Culture and Center for the Study of Immigrant Integration hosted Susan Coutin during a sabbatical that was devoted to working on the manuscript.

Our deepest debt of gratitude goes to the individuals who were willing to be interviewed for our research or who shared their lives with us, and to the organizations with which we collaborated, including the Central American Resource Center in Los Angeles and Sweden's Adoption Centre.

We thank visual artist Jill Holslin for permission to reproduce the piece *Escalera*, from the series *Testing Trump's Wall*, 2017. We are also grateful to artist Tucker Nichols for permission to reproduce his drawing *Must Be Can't Be Real*, which originally appeared in "What Does Quantum Physics Actually Tell Us about the World?"—James Gleick's May 8, 2018, *New York Times* review of Adam Becker's *What Is Real?*

While the majority of *Documenting Impossible Realities* is original material, we do draw on and revise limited excerpts of our own previously published material. Chapter 3 is a revised version of our coauthored article from 2008, "Schrödinger's Cat and the Ethnography of Law" (*PoLAR: Political and Legal Anthropology Review* 31 [1]: 61–78). Our discussion of memory in chapter 1 draws on several paragraphs from Susan Coutin's *Exiled Home: Salvadoran Transnational Youth in the Aftermath of Violence*, published by Duke University Press in 2016. In addition, some of the interview material we quote in this book has appeared in *Exiled Home*. *Documenting Impossible Realities* also includes adapted excerpts from longer interviews with three transnational adoptees that appear in chapters 5, 6, and 7 of Barbara Yngvesson's *Belonging in an Adopted*

World: Race, Identity, and Transnational Adoption, published by the University of Chicago Press in 2010. We include this material with the permission of the University of Chicago Press.

Our research over the years benefited from the involvement of research assistants, including Véronique Fortin and Gray Abarca for Susan, and Laura Ring for Barbara.

The manuscript was much improved by our conversations with colleagues, some of whom read portions of the draft and provided written feedback. We thank Gray Abarca, Beth Baker, Victoria Bernal, Michelle Bigenho, Tom Boellstorff, Lee Cabatingan, Heath Cabot, Pooja Dadhania, David Engel, Gisela Fosado, Ilana Gershon, David Goldberg, Carol Greenhouse, Sora Han, Julie Hemment, Eleana Kim, Lynn Mather, Bill Maurer, Sally Merry, Beth Mertz, Julie Mitchell, Alison Mountz, Beth Notar, Christina Platt, Keramet Reiter, Justin Richland, Annelise Riles, Maura Roessner, Carrie Rosenbaum, Joshua Roth, Judith Schachter, Gabi Schwab, Nomi Stolzenberg, Franz von Benda Beckman, Keebet von Benda Beckman, Peter Wissoker, and Mei Zhan. David Engel's careful reading of a draft of Chapter 1 was especially helpful. Conversations with students and former students also informed our analysis, particularly Gray Abarca, Alyse Bertenthal, Josh Clark, Véronique Fortin, Gabriela Gonzalez, Kristen Maziarka, Jason Palmer, Justin Perez, Kasey Ragan, Jo Resnick, Laura Ring, Liz Rubio, Daina Sanchez, Linda Sanchez, Erica Vogel, and the members of UC Irvine's Law and Ethnography Lab. For Susan, conversations with the postdoctoral scholars Angie Fillingim, Jessica López-Espino, and Caitlin Patler were also important. For Barbara, conversations with Sara Nordin, Anna Chuchu Schindele, and Hanna Wallensteen over the years in which this research was conducted provided important insights.

Earlier versions of portions of the manuscript were presented at the Law and Society Association Annual Meeting, the UC Humanities Research Institute, the Clarke Center for International and Comparative Legal Studies at Cornell Law School, the Oñati International Institute for the Sociology of Law, the Annual Meeting of the American Ethnological Society, and the American Anthropological Association. We are grateful to discussants, fellow panelists, and audience members for their critical feedback.

We also would like to thank our editor, Jim Lance, as well as the editorial staff at Cornell University Press. We are grateful for their support and for everything they did to bring this book to fruition.

We could not have produced this book without the support of our families: Curt Coutin, Jesse Coutin, Jordy Coutin, Raphael Coutin, Casey Coutin, Dag Yngvesson, Finn Yngvesson, and Sigfrid Yngvesson. Dag Yngvesson read and commented on portions of our manuscript, and we are especially indebted to Sigfrid Yngvesson for reviewing our discussions of quantum physics.

"WHAT LIES BACK OF THE WORK"

In August 2012, one of us—Susan—met with Carlos, a twenty-year-old recent high school graduate who was applying for Deferred Action for Childhood Arrivals (DACA) at a Los Angeles nonprofit where Susan was doing fieldwork and volunteer work. The name "Carlos" is a pseudonym; indeed, throughout this manuscript, Susan used pseudonyms for individuals she encountered during fieldwork, whereas Barbara generally has not used pseudonyms. At the time, the DACA program was in its earliest days. DACA had been created by the Obama administration in June 2012 to provide temporary relief from deportation for young adults who had grown up in the United States but were undocumented. To qualify for DACA, these so-called child arrivals had to prove that they had entered the United States before their sixteenth birthday; had been in the United States continuously from June 15, 2007, to the time of their application submission; were either enrolled in or graduates of high school; and had a clean criminal record. In addition, applicants had to be physically present in the United States on June 15, 2012 (the date the program was initiated), and at the time of their application. Successful DACA applicants would receive a work permit and permission to remain in the United States for two years but would not be granted legal status. Between June 2012, when DACA was announced, and August 2012, when the application period opened, would-be applicants scrambled to assemble the necessary documentation to prove eligibility. Likewise, organizations such as the nonprofit where Susan was doing fieldwork trained new volunteers, hired additional staff, tried to anticipate the application form and evidentiary requirements, held informational sessions, and reorganized to serve the thousands who were expected to apply. In this context of heightened need, Susan pitched in to help out as a volunteer. Carlos's DACA application was the second one she worked on.

Susan began the appointment by explaining that she was a volunteer and asked to see the documents that Carlos had brought with him. Carlos pulled out a folder in which he had gathered his documents, and Susan began making a pile of documents relevant to each of the DACA eligibility requirements. She learned that Carlos had graduated from high school in June 2011. He had a passport, a birth certificate, vaccination records, a high school diploma, transcripts, school records (report cards and awards), copies of his school IDs going back to elementary school, and a letter regarding volunteer service that he had performed during spring and summer 2012. Looking these over, Susan saw proof of his current age (birth certificate and passport), proof of entry before his sixteenth birthday (school records), and proof of schooling (diploma). The only problem she saw was proof of continuous presence. He had proof of the years from 2007 to 2011 through his school records, each of which covered an entire year. But for the time since graduation, he had only the volunteer service letter, which meant he had no record to prove presence from June 2011 to April 2012.

Susan consulted with a staff member, who identified two problems: (1) the documentation gap was too long, almost a year; and (2) US immigration officials had said that circumstantial evidence was insufficient to prove presence in the United States on June 15, 2012. The volunteer service letter was circumstantial evidence, so Carlos would need additional documentation.

Carlos told Susan that he could get copies of sign-in sheets to document his volunteer service during the missing months. But documentation of presence on June 15, 2012, could be challenging. He explained that he lived with his parents, so he did not have any bills in his name; he did not have his own bank account; and, since graduation, he had worked only odd jobs, such as cutting the neighbors' grass. Then, as he was about to leave, Carlos asked, "What about receipts from Game Stop?" He said that he had reserved video games that were about to come out and ultimately purchased them. That activity had generated receipts with both his name and the date. "It might have saved me," Carlos commented as he left, planning to return for a future appointment with the additional documentation.

More than a decade earlier, in the spring of 1998, one of us—Barbara—accompanied a group of adoptees from Chile and their Swedish adoptive parents on a "roots trip" that would take them from Santiago in the north to Temuco in southern Chile. The trip included visits to hospitals, orphanages, and a family court, where the relinquishment of most of the adoptees by their birth mothers had been finalized in the early 1980s. In addition, organizers had planned reunions with foster mothers who had cared for the adoptees before their departure for Sweden almost two decades previously, a meeting with the doctor who had delivered many of them, and a meeting with social workers who had been involved in the adoptions. The trip concluded with a formal ceremony in Santiago during which the director of the Servicio Nacional de Menores (National Service of Minors, or SENAME)—the Chilean child welfare service—in an emotional moment, told the assembled participants that Chile was their country. Barbara, who was conducting fieldwork at Sweden's nonprofit Adoption Centre at the time, was asked to serve as a Swedish–Spanish interpreter on the trip. The adoptees, who were in their teens and early twenties, had been adopted in the late 1970s and early 1980s, during the dictatorship of Augusto Pinochet, and this was their first return to Chile since the adoption. The trip also constituted a kind of return for the Swedish adoption organization through which the adoptees had been placed, since Chile had suspended transnational adoptions in 1991 in the context of reported irregularities in the procurement of children in that country toward the end of Pinochet's rule, and the official and unofficial structures and relations supporting transnational adoption in the country were dismantled.[1] Preparations for the roots trip thus involved what one of the organizers described as "true detective work" to unearth the networks through which Chilean adoptive children circulated on their journey to becoming Swedish people.

Maria, a sixteen-year-old adoptee, explained that she had wondered before making the trip, "Do I really come from Chile?" Unlike a friend who was adopted from Colombia, whom Maria described as "having more of a Mapuche-like appearance," she was not obviously "from Latin America." With her light skin, "I could have been something else," she explained, referring to her experience growing up in Sweden. By the end of the trip, however, Maria's sense of connection to Chile was much more focused. Recalling the moment at the closing ceremony when the director of SENAME told the group, "This is your country," Maria said, "It was, I think it was for everyone, it was a conviction that, 'OK, I am from Chile, too!' It was like a confirmation from a Chilean and from the country itself that I am from Chile. It was so big in some way. That was why we dared to respond and began to cry."

Similarly, Clara, an eighteen-year-old who was accompanied on the trip by her adoptive mother, described an evening gathering with the foster mothers who had cared for the adoptees before they were sent to Sweden as the moment when "I began to realize that I was really there." She had fantasized about Chile before the trip, but "it felt strange to be there. It felt as though I myself was left in Sweden although my body was in Chile, and so was somewhere in between, where one didn't know where one was. It was really strange. But when we met the foster mothers, I found myself." Like Maria, whose light skin made her wonder if she really came from Chile, Clara had worried at times about who she was, but in her case, it was her dark skin that occasioned doubts. She recalled a time in the second grade when some people came up to her and began speaking Spanish, and she "couldn't grasp what they were saying. And then I began to think, 'They see me as an immigrant, when actually I am Swedish.' And you know, sometimes I forget that I am dark-skinned. When I sit with friends and chat. And then when I look in the mirror: 'Aha! That's how it is!'"

This sudden sense of "Aha!" was intensified on the roots trip to Chile and was a key element in the repeated (re)discovery by adoptees that one is not "completely Swedish." This discovery was mediated, in part, by its collective dimension and by the support experienced from other adoptees and from adoptive parents. As Clara explained, regarding the close bonds developed among adoptees on the trip, "One didn't need to explain how one felt, because everyone felt the same." This same feeling was on the one hand exhilarating, as it involved a kind of grounding of an intuited self as Chilean that had always seemed just out of reach in Sweden. On the other hand, the experience of grounding was complicated by the impossibility of separating being Chilean (of being dark-skinned, of being "Mapuche-like") from the reality of abandonment that was rediscovered in the physical spaces of hospitals, orphanages, and courtrooms; in the spoken words of social workers and government officials; and in the writing on documents that finalized the separation of each adoptee from their mother and from the country to which they were now returning in order to find or know themselves.

The carefully cultivated experience of pride in being Chilean, transmitted by the Swedish parents of the adoptees and connected to these adoptive parents' experience of the trip as "my life's trip," was contingent on the adoptees' displacement to Sweden and on their being able to imagine Chile in the way their adoptive parents did—as part of a tour of Chile or a temporary visit from afar. Adoptees could share this imagined Chile with their adoptive parents, but the parents could only act as witnesses to a Chile that their children had once experienced firsthand and up close. This complex, emotionally explosive Chile was in the rooms and beds of an orphanage where Maria had spent several months as an infant, in the feel and smell of a rosary that belonged to Clara's mother and was given to her in a meeting just before the end of the tour, and in the written words and physical presence of a doctor or matron who had recorded the details of a particular child's delivery. As one twenty-year-old woman described her feelings after reading through a file of documents at the Temuco court, visiting the orphanage where she had spent three weeks as an infant, and driving by the house where her birth mother once lived, "It was the most tumultuous day of my life; I found out about everything!"

Just as Carlos struggled to document his presence in the United States following his graduation from high school, so that he could complete his DACA application, so too did the adoption organization that planned the roots trip to Chile struggle to put together what was in effect a challenging puzzle that would connect the Swedish adoptees to their origins in Chile. This challenge was an effect of the irregularities that troubled Swedish adoptions from that country and that came to light both on the roots trip and in the second decade of the 2000s. A key issue was the slippage between the finalization of the adoptions in Sweden once the children arrived in that country, and their registration in the Chilean civil registry with the names of their adoptive parents once their relinquishment was finalized in the Temuco court. In effect, the "Chilean child" disappeared on paper before even leaving the country, but the children who were to be adopted had left traces: in photographs, in the memories of foster mothers and unofficial records of doctors, and in the sealed documents they were allowed to hold and read at the Temuco court, where they had been relinquished. The goal of the roots trip was to reconnect the adoptees on the trip to this "disappeared" past by bringing it into the present in various ways, and in one case by mediating the meeting of one of the adoptees, Clara, with her birth mother, whose child had been, as one social worker at the Temuco court put it, "dead to her" for eighteen years. In that case, not only was the meeting with her disappeared mother key to Clara, but arguably no less significant for her was the rosary that her birth mother gave her during this meeting and about which she commented in an interview a month later: "I could see that it had been used, and it had a special smell. It smelled like her." It was "something one knows about that one can make something of [later], on one's own."

By bringing our research on unauthorized movement and transnational adoption into conversation with each other, as we have through these vignettes, the text that follows puts forward a vision of documentation that is informed by our experiences as legal anthropologists.[2] Juxtaposing our work in this fashion enabled us to see the fields in which we and other ethnographers are immersed as unfixed, constituted in relationships with interlocutors, and moving with ethnographers through their fieldnotes and memories, rather than simply being there to be inhabited. Immersion within such unfixed fields produces *fieldsight*, a kind of binocular vision made possible by being entangled in two realities that are incompatible but that also must be true—such as the notion that an immigrant such as Carlos is both unauthorized and a member of society, or that birth mothers and children such as Maria and Clara are kin yet unrelated. Exploring such incompatible realities ethnographically has meant paying attention to the "as if"—that is, to illusion and fantasy in the making of shared representations of reality. Thus, those who are citizens by birth act as if they belong in national territories, biological parents act as if their family relations are natural, and ethnographers act as if they are researchers rather than merely volunteers or interpreters. Such claims to truth are dependent on and therefore entangled with other realities that are considered only approximations, such as insights produced by those who are not researchers, naturalization, and creating a family through adoption. Each of these approximations of truth—an ethnographic account, an award of citizenship, an adoptive family—is threatened by a canceled or hidden past: the time before a researcher's arrival, immigrants' relationships to their countries of origin, an adopted child's relationship to birth parents. To theorize such relationships between seemingly disparate yet inseparable moments, we have drawn on notions of entanglement that we derived from multiple disciplines. These include critical ethnography's claim that ethnographers are not outside the fields that they inhabit, object relations theory's contention that external realities and internal states of being cannot always be distinguished, and quantum physics' discovery that particles that are light-years away from one another are somehow nonetheless connected. Our exploration of entanglement between official and unofficial realities led us to consider experiences of political disappearances and exile in addition to transnational adoption and unauthorized immigration. Examining entanglement in these examples sheds light on relationships, processes that are in the middle, and a sort of in-betweenness that cannot be pinned down, such as being absent but present, alive yet dead, or a participant who is also observing.

The account of documentation that we develop here speaks to the current historical moment, in which the structural relationship between the aboveground world inhabited by dominant groups and the underground realm to which unauthorized immigrants and political exiles are relegated is unstable and shifting. This relationship, which is made possible by the illusions that some people do not belong, that some forms of kin are not real, or that certain ways of knowing do not count, both holds societies together and tears them apart.[3] The United States has just lived through a period in which essential workers who have performed critical in-person labor during the COVID-19 pandemic may be undocumented. Moreover, this structural relationship is not new. US employers have a long history of hiring workers who are vulnerable to deportation and who are therefore more exploitable. Undocumented workers, transnational adoptees, and many others whose lives defy social conventions experience documentation challenges. They may be continually asked to prove who they are, may find themselves misrepresented or absent in official records and popular accounts, and may seek creative ways of documenting their own histories and desired futures. To explore the tension that lies at the heart of living incompatible yet entangled realities (unauthorized workers who are essential laborers, family members who are and are not kin), we do not focus on a single group of people, as might a traditional ethnography; rather, we explore the space *between* groups and the ways that each haunts the other: native born citizens may fear that immigrants will change citizens' ways of life, people may wonder whether or not they actually were adopted, and both immigrants and transnational adoptees may be produced through political violence.[4] Exploring the space between realities requires collaboration, both with each other and with interlocutors, whose words we take seriously as theoretical insights in their own right.[5] We likewise attend to accounts produced by filmmakers, displayed in museum exhibits, enacted in plays, or published as memoirs. By juxtaposing and moving between entangled realities and modes of expression, we attempt to convey the emotional experience of oscillating between being here and gone, between being legitimate and treated as counterfeit. We anticipate that students and junior scholars will find that this approach resonates with their own experiences, as they have had to develop means of learning and producing knowledge in fraught contexts where there is a heightened awareness of racial violence and injustice, or where educational achievement may also be experienced as something that creates distance from one's own community and past.

Documenting Impossible Realities is informed by an ethnographic sensibility but is not a traditional ethnography in the sense of explicating a particular cultural process, group, or phenomenon. Rather, the book's structure reflects a relational approach in that we juxtapose vivid examples in ways that we hope will inspire readers' imaginations and thinking. Thus, our collaboration extends to our audience. We employ a writing style that has been referred to as "collaging," an assemblage whose meaning is greater than the sum of its parts.[6] In contrast to more linear narratives, we move around temporally, bringing forward snippets of earlier writing, returning to prior moments in our own fieldwork, and considering alternatives that have not—or not yet—been realized. For example, the opening to this prologue draws on fieldwork experiences from the 1990s and the 2010s. At the same time, there is a logic to the ordering of chapters. We begin in chapter 1 by considering entanglements between realities that have been defined as "counterfeited" and those defined as "true" or "natural," an interrelationship that gives rise to potential spaces that cannot be pinned down. For example, Carlos was regarded as an outsider who lacked documentation but also as a child arrival who deserved humanitarian consideration because he was "like" other Americans. In chapter 2 we explore fieldsight, the vantage point created by looking within and from these spaces. For instance, the roots trip positioned Maria and Clara within and outside of both Sweden and Chile at the same time. Next, chapter 3 explores how such fieldsight makes it possible to see what is in the middle—that is, what has not yet been resolved into a discovery that is found or an invention that is created, as when

Clara struggled to see herself as both Swedish and dark-skinned. In chapter 4 we turn to the searching that is part of research that attempts to transcend divisions between a past that has been cut off, a present that cannot be fully realized, and a future that has already been encountered. For example, we consider how Chilean women whose relatives were disappeared during the last dictatorship search for their relatives' remains, keeping their memories alive in hopes of a future encounter with this hidden past. We conclude in chapter 5 by examining what Einstein termed "spooky action at a distance," namely the effects of entanglement on the relationship between seemingly impossible realities—particles that are separated by millions of miles and nonetheless influence each other (in quantum theory), or a past that has been cut off but nonetheless makes itself felt in the present (in legal ethnography).[7] Our analysis thus comes full circle; indeed, we hope that because our book is shorter than most, readers will be able to juxtapose each chapter, experiencing the text immersively.

Our relational approach to ethnography is simultaneously a relational approach to law as a fiction that creates and entangles impossible realities. We see both space and time in relational terms; that is, instead of being bounded, spaces intersect, and instead of being linear, time can be retroactive. For instance, Sweden and Chile intersected during the 1998 roots trip, and Carlos's DACA application process required retroactively assessing his life in the United States as grounds for work authorization and temporary permission to remain in the country. Our perspective contrasts with that of legal scholars who have distinguished between law on the books (written law) and law in action (how law is put into practice, which may not align with written statutes). We see both space and time as infused with legal meaning, so law is not inert (law on the books) or existing primarily in practices (law in action) but is rather *alive-dead*, an oscillating state according to which legal constructs such as citizenship, parentage, or rights can be produced after the fact and in ways that are tied to locations. Examples of such legal oscillations include US immigration law, which can separate parents and children based on the claim that they are unrelated; adoption law, which erases the identities of children who are adopted; or human rights law, which can define persecution victims who flee their countries as undeserving of refuge. By exploring the as ifs that animate these and other relationships, we bring readers along a journey through what must be yet cannot be real.

COUNTERFEITING REALITY

Legal Fictions and the Construction
of Everyday Belongings

> **At the very beginning, fantasy is not a substitute for reality, but the first method of finding it.**
>
> Adam Phillips, *Winnicott*

> **All "phenomena" are literally "appearances."**
>
> Gregory Bateson, *Steps to an Ecology of Mind*

This is a book about displaced populations and the powerful emotional effects of their dislocations, both on the people directly involved and on others. It is also a book about the contingency of belonging and the legal fictions that authorize belonging as if it were a natural state that precedes its legal documentation. Our focus is on the challenges that such fictions pose to those who are positioned on the threshold of multiple potential belongings, none of which can be fully realized. These challenges are widespread, as dislocation is experienced by a range of people, such as those who are forced out of their countries of origin by political violence, poverty, or climate change; those whose lives are disrupted by a catastrophe; residents who are forced to move due to gentrification; families forever altered by a tragedy or an unexpected event; even students who are caught between the world of the university and their communities of origin. In these and other circumstances, belonging may be called into question or may be defined in ways that are experienced as alienating. While we focus on particular examples in this book, we hope that our analysis will resonate more broadly with those who have experienced some form of impossible realities.

In *Documenting Impossible Realities*, we ask, How do the experiences of adoptees, deportees, migrants, and other exilic populations reveal the limitations of conventional accounts through which belonging is documented? What image of reality appears if we foreground its counterfeited forms—the as-if-begotten child in an adoptive family; the undocumented who are forced to live as if they are legal citizens; politically disappeared individuals whose relatives insist that their lives cannot be erased? And how might grasping the real through its approximations affect the ways we understand the production of ethnographic truth claims? While our focus is on exilic peoples, one of our key points is that biological kin, citizens by birth or descent, and those who remain in their countries of origin *also* exist in multiple worlds, even though this may not be apparent to them.[1]

This book grows out of a twenty-year collaboration in which we have examined the common assumptions underlying two seemingly different forms of displacement: *transnational adoption*, in which displacement from national territory is officially made to disappear and the individual's adopted status is treated as the only official reality, and *unauthorized movement*, in which an individual's displacement from one country to another is treated as the only thing that defines that individual's reality (as undocumented). Each of these processes draws attention to the dislocations that characterize the contemporary era, the key role of movement in everyday life, and the ways that dislocation can be understood as spatializing personhood. What we mean when we say that dislocation "spatializes" personhood is that for those who are unauthorized and those who are adopted, belonging is disrupted; home is insecure; and personhood is defined by the as ifs that inevitably haunt it: the child who might have been me, the country that could have been mine, the person I might have become. Engaging ethnographically with transnational adoption and unauthorized movement, as with other forms of exile, calls for approaches that are attentive to the fictional quality of everyday life, the experienced fraudulence of a reality that is threatened by a canceled past, and the key role of evidentiary records in distinguishing licit from illicit realities. Bringing our ethnographic analyses of adoption and immigration together reveals the subtexts that link adoptees and migrants to their (unauthorized) beginnings and the common histories of violence underlying their (in)voluntary removal from the countries where they were born. To attend to these common histories of violence, we also consider political disappearances and the lives in exile to which they give rise. Such experiences are not rare, given the pervasiveness of migration, political violence, and as-if families. Indeed, violence, global inequalities, and disrupted belongings are central themes within ethnic studies, critical studies, and feminism; and understanding such processes is key to advancing social justice.

To provide examples of these issues of dislocation, violence, and irreality, we turn now to two cases, one a class action brought by the American Civil Liberties Union against US Immigration and Customs Enforcement in 2018, the other a formal petition filed with the Riksdag (Swedish parliament) by the Association of Ethiopian and Eritrean Adoptees in Stockholm in 2018.

Case 1

In February 2018, the American Civil Liberties Union brought a class action against US Immigration and Customs Enforcement (ICE) and other government agencies on behalf of asylum seekers. At issue in this case was ICE officials' widespread practice of separating undocumented children and parents so that the latter could be prosecuted for entering the United States without authorization or detained while their immigration cases were pending. ICE officials justified such separations by arguing that there was no evidence that the adults in question were actually the children's parents, that the parents may have been unfit, and that the facilities where the adults were being held were not appropriate for children. One such separation was experienced by a woman described in court records as Ms. L., a Congolese asylum seeker and the lead plaintiff in the case. According to court records, Ms. L. and her six-year-old daughter, S.S., presented themselves at a US port of entry in 2017 and requested asylum. They were detained, and a few days later, S.S. was taken away from Ms. L., crying and begging to remain with her mother. As the judge in this case wrote, "Immigration officials claimed they had concerns whether Ms. L. was S.S.'s mother, despite Ms. L.'s protestations to the contrary and S.S.'s behavior."[2] Ms. L. was placed in expedited removal proceedings, which converted S.S. into an "unaccompanied minor" under the jurisdiction of the Office of Refugee Resettlement (ORR). ORR placed S.S. in a facility in Chicago, more than a thousand miles away from Ms. L. After determining that Ms. L had a credible fear of persecution in her home country, officials placed her in removal proceedings, where she could pursue her asylum claim. She was released from detention after the lawsuit was filed but was not reunited with S.S. until after a court-ordered DNA test confirmed that she was S.S.'s biological parent. S.S. and Ms. L. had been separated for approximately five months and were permitted to speak over the phone only six times during that time. According to court documents, some two thousand families went through similar separations.[3]

The experiences of Ms. L. and S.S. were part of an international controversy over the Trump administration's zero tolerance policy, which required all adults who were apprehended while entering the United States without authorization to be prosecuted, regardless of whether they were seeking asylum or traveling with a child.[4] Official skepticism about noncitizens' claimed kin relationships is not unusual, however. US citizens and lawful permanent residents (LPRs) who petition the US government for a visa for a spouse who is not a US citizen or an LPR must go to great lengths to prove that their marriages are not fraudulent.[5] Couples must assemble photographs of their wedding and their daily lives, declarations detailing their love for each other, letters of support from friends and relatives who know them as a couple, birth records of any children they have had together, bank statements showing that their finances are shared, jointly filed tax returns, rental contracts with both of their names on the lease, and more.[6] Additionally, if an officer suspects marriage fraud during the first interview, couples can then be interviewed separately by officials who will attempt to catch discrepancies in their accounts. Fathers who file visa petitions for children born out of wedlock must prove their relationship through blood ties, DNA tests, records of financial support, and evidence of emotional relationships. Even siblings sometimes face challenges.[7] Undocumented kin relationships also occur in the case of international adoption.

Case 2

In February 2018, the Association of Ethiopian and Eritrean Adoptees (AEF) in Stockholm brought a formal petition to the Swedish parliament, distributing copies to relevant government offices and other international adoptee associations, requesting what they described as a "paradigm shift in Sweden's approach to international adoptions."[8] Opening with "Adoption begins with an adoption process but an adoptee's life begins at birth," the petition declared that international adoptees "are not blank slates who were born at Arlanda [the Stockholm airport]. We have biological parents, just as everyone else does."[9] The petition called for the implementation of stringent policies in Sweden and in the nations from which Sweden receives children in adoption to ensure the preservation of all possible information regarding why a decision was made to place a child in international adoption rather than in the custody of relatives or adoptive parents in the country of birth. Such policies could provide "a key link for many adoptees who search for their roots as a way of piecing together a clearer picture of themselves and their history."[10] A month later, AEF submitted a second document to the Swedish parliament and the other parties calling for Sweden to immediately change adoption policy to bring the country into conformity with the UN Convention on the Rights of the Child.[11] Petitioners were concerned specifically with article 8 of the convention, which addresses children's right to preserve their identity, "including nationality, name and family relations as recognized by law without unlawful interference."[12]

At issue in these official petitions from AEF was Sweden's and other nations' widespread policy of establishing a legal "clean break" between children to be adopted by families in these countries and children's birth family and nation.[13] Rationalized by the presumption that it was in the child's best interest to be completely integrated into the adopting family and country, the policy was implemented by designating children who might be eligible for international adoption as legal orphans in their country of birth (regardless of whether they had living parents) and as the "as-if-begotten" children of their new parents in the adopting country.[14] The second AEF petition cited recent revelations in the Swedish press of "the fabrication of parentless children" from Ethiopia, Eritrea, Chile, and India, and the transfer of these children to Sweden for legal adoption—practices that challenged Sweden's reputation in the twentieth century as a strong advocate for children's rights in the international arena.[15]

Sara, a founding member of AEF, described the emotional complexity of what an adoptive identity requires: "You have to prove, both for yourself and others, that you are Swedish, because you have [in my case] this Ethiopianness [*det här etiopiska*] that is such an irritating presence."[16] Only when she returned to Addis Ababa as an adult and found her name in the registry of the Kebebe Tsehay orphanage, from which she was adopted, did Ethiopia take shape as an emotional reality for her. As Sara explained, "I think that before you develop a relationship to Ethiopia, there is a part of you that you know is a part, but you don't know what it is. But when you begin to find a way to relate to that, then you can also take [for granted] the other, the Swedish, because then it is up to you whether you want to be Swedish or Ethiopian, or whatever you want to do about that." Another woman, Amanda, recounted how once she'd located her birth parents and begun a series of return trips to Ethiopia, adoption became a charged topic in her family, particularly in her relationship with her Swedish mother. On the eve of her fourth trip to Ethiopia, in the early 2000s, her Swedish mother told her that she had begun to fear "that I would become transfixed by my feelings and by Ethiopia. But I told her that I can't be transfixed by it. It is the reality I live in. It isn't that I create something that doesn't exist."[17]

Impossible Realities

In these examples, Ms. L., S.S., individuals seeking to petition for their relatives to immigrate to the United States, and members of the AEF, such as Sara and Amanda, experienced impossible realities—that is, versions of their selves, relationships, histories, and futures that were incompatible with each other and therefore could not all be true but that were nonetheless experienced or treated as real. In one version of reality, Ms. L. and S.S. were relatives who had traveled to the United States together, while in another, their claim to be related was deemed fraudulent and S.S. was an unaccompanied minor. Similarly, transnational adoptees in Sweden had to contend with being completely Swedish yet Ethiopian or

Eritrean, orphans who had living birth families, immigrants whose lives began in Sweden, people whose histories preceded their origin, individuals whose pasts were in some ways determined by their futures.

Complex racial, gendered, and global inequalities undergird these impossible realities. Ms. L., a Congolese asylum seeker, was affected by the nationalist and nativist policies that have increased detentions, separated families, and excluded those in search of refuge in the United States. Likewise, Sara's sense of Ethiopia as an "irritating presence" in her life was linked to racial politics in Sweden, where her Blackness marked her as "not Swedish" even though she was a naturalized Swedish citizen and Swedish adoption law had canceled her relationship to Ethiopia. Moreover, these dynamics, which pervade international relations and have deep historical roots, are not easy to pin down as internal or external to individuals. Here, the as-if dimension of immigrant-ness is made visible by adoptive bodies even as Swedish-ness becomes as if when embodied by adoptees.[18]

The gulfs in understanding that make realities both real and impossible provoke intense, sometimes violent emotions. Amanda described her relationship with her birth family in Ethiopia as "the reality I live in," a reality that includes her family in Sweden but that her adoptive mother finds threatening. The United States' claims to be protecting children through family separations, or the notion that a child's best interests *require* a legal clean break, are belied by the experiences of the affected families, even as these families' relatedness may have been legally constructed or canceled.

The porous borders between that which is natural, unauthorized, or adopted in these examples point to the instabilities of belonging and the seeming arbitrariness with which entities are realized in one form or another. Such shapeshifting hints as well at the possibility that belongings are always in process, never complete, held in place by complex social and legal fictions that authorize only certain forms of belonging as real. Here we underscore the power of legal fictions—the as-if-begotten child who is legally "disappeared" from her birth family (and country) of origin and made to legally "originate" in her adoptive family and nation; the as-if citizen who was supposedly "illegal" all along because her parents failed to take the needed legal steps to naturalize her.[19] Fictionalizing acts such as these are key in constructing not only those who are adopted or unauthorized but also so-called natural belongings.[20] Familiar narratives of a "normal" world populated by the native born, who do not require making into citizens; of families that do not require making by law; and of subjects who do not require legal identification begin to seem phantasmic, contingent on the work of figures like the immigrant and the adoptee for their realization.[21] This contingency of licit on illicit belongings makes the so-called natural world begin to "shimmer" and look "uncannily like what psychoanalysis would call an 'as if' phenomenon."[22]

Ethnography as Entanglement

> Any time two entities interact, they entangle. . . . In doing so, they lose their separate existence. No matter how far they move apart, if one is tweaked, measured, observed, the other seems instantly to respond, even if the whole world now lies between them.
>
> Louisa Gilder, *The Age of Entanglement*

> Entanglement is the strangest of all strange quantum phenomena, the one that takes us furthest away from our old understanding of the world. But it is also something general, which in a sense weaves the very structure of reality.
>
> Rovelli, *Helgoland*

In exploring how connections between seemingly incompatible realities trouble distinctions between inside and outside and across space and time, we bring our own ethnographic work on transnational adoption and unauthorized migration into conversation with other works that document what legal scholar Mae Ngai refers to as an "impossible subject": "a person who cannot be and a problem that cannot be solved."[23] The works we consider include not only ethnography but such genres as autoethnography, documentary film, memoir, theater performance, museum installations, and other forms of documentation that focuses on dislocation, including legal or physical disappearance and its powerful emotional effects. These works are interconnected in that political violence displaces people, potentially leading to emigration and exile, and such dislocations can include the abduction of children who are adopted into other families. Our own research has therefore engaged political disappearances either directly, through Susan's work on political asylum, or indirectly, through Barbara's work on adoption, in that political violence and human rights abuses are part of the broader context that makes children "available" for transnational adoption.[24] In each of the works we consider, the narrator, author, ethnographer, artist, or filmmaker is positioned at the intersection of incompatible worlds (e.g., the worlds of inner and outer reality, of memory and the everyday, of licit and illicit domains). This positioning may be an effect of physical dislocation (as in cases of deportation, adoption, abduction, or other forms of exile) and may produce emotional dislocation (as in the experiences of adoptees who return to their countries of origin to discover that they had other families all along, as we discuss in chapters 2 and 3, or in the experiences of US transnational adoptees who discover as adults that they have been undocumented all along because their parents failed to naturalize them). For ethnographers, the truth claims of ethnography are both discovered and invented in such breaches between worlds.

We have found anthropologist Roy Wagner's concept of "counterfeiting reality" helpful as a metaphor for capturing the dynamic of licit and illicit belongings, not only in the experiences of unauthorized persons, those who are adopted, and other exilic populations, but also—as previously suggested—in the everyday practices of ethnographers such as ourselves, who seek to document impossible lives.[25] Wagner understands counterfeiting as a kind of "invention through objectification" in which the fieldworker "creates the subject in the act of trying to represent it more objectively, and simultaneously creates (through analogous extension) the ideas and forms through which it is invented."[26] In a related approach, anthropologist Jean Jackson explores ethnography's ability to approximate the real.[27] Through interviews with seventy field researchers about the emotional dimensions of their relationship to fieldnotes, Jackson focuses on the ways that fieldnotes are thought to simultaneously reflect and create reality. Fieldnotes, Jackson suggests, "are a 'translation' but are still en route from an internal and other-cultural state to a final destination."[28] In this sense, fieldnotes occupy a liminal space "between reality and thesis, between memory and publication, between training and professional life."[29] Ethnographers must immerse themselves in the field yet cannot fully do so; the field is real yet is delimited in part by the ethnographer; ethnographic accounts are constructed by ethnographers yet also grounded in observations. Ethnographers' location at this intersection between reality and its shadowy counterpart—a location that was key in the research that each of us has conducted—gives ethnographers a kind of double vision, a theme we take up in chapter 2. Ethnography is in this sense intrinsically relational, not only in that it is carried out through interpersonal relationships but also in that it is positioned at the interface of entangled worlds, even if there are times when only one of them is visible.

Our account of the place of ethnography in documenting entangled worlds brings classical and more recent approaches to ethnographic practice into conversation with quantum physics and psychoanalytic theory. We draw on anthropologist Gregory Bateson's ecological approach to social reality as a system in which difference, or dimensionality, is understood as an effect of binocular vision, which provides the seer/observer with information "about the world around itself or about itself as a part of that external world."[30] Bateson criticized linear logics for failing to take interdependence and feedback loops into account, noting that his "ultimate goal in an inquiry is the larger pattern which connects."[31] Bateson therefore examined not only figure but ground, not only what was visible but what had to be intuited, as well as the framings that direct attention to one and away from the other. The as if is one such framing in that it productively entangles otherwise incompatible realities: real–not real, field–not field, kin–non-kin, citizen–noncitizen.[32] We find Bateson's work particularly germane to understanding the fieldsight generated through such relationships.[33]

We also draw on the work of anthropologist Aimee Meredith Cox, who examines the larger pattern that connects the truth as described or performed by young low-income Black women living in a Detroit homeless shelter with "the truth you don't see on TV or in the papers."[34] Focusing on "the complicated interplay of external and self-evaluations fueled by the representational work of labels and tropes hurled at them from multiple points of origin," Cox provides a nuanced exploration of what one of her interlocutors termed the "missing middle" that constitutes "truth" for Black girls at the shelter.[35] From her position as a witness to their experiences, Cox developed an understanding of her subjects as "shapeshifters," arguing that they were not simply units of analysis whose lives needed "sanitizing, normalizing, rectifying, or translating." Rather, she argues, ethnographers, caseworkers, TV reporters, board members of the shelter, and others who judge these women on a daily basis must "open [them]selves to a conversation with them, with the full expectation that [they] will, at least, be changed."[36]

Cox's approach recalls Saba Mahmood's discussion of "rendering the other," in which Mahmood argues for "analysis as a mode of conversation, rather than mastery, [which] can yield a vision of coexistence that does not require making others' lifeworlds extinct or provisional."[37] Both Cox and Mahmood, in turn, remind us of critical legal theorist Patricia Williams's path-breaking book *Alchemy of Race and Rights*, in which Williams promotes a technique of legal analysis that "can serve to describe a community of context for those social actors whose traditional legal status has been the isolation of oxymoron, of oddity, of outsider." Williams argues for a genre of writing "that reveals the intersubjectivity of legal constructions, that forces the reader both to participate in the construction of meaning and to be conscious of that process."[38]

Our own analytical approach focuses on this community of context and the "multivalent ways of seeing" it engenders by drawing on the work of object relations theorist D. W. Winnicott.[39] Winnicott deepens our understanding of ethnography as entanglement by theorizing the complex play of visible and invisible, licit and illicit, and exterior and interior realities that constitutes the world in which people live. Best known for his approach to object relations as a dynamic process of "keeping inner and outer reality separate yet interrelated," Winnicott explores this dynamic by positing that "transitional objects" (a blanket, a soft toy, or some other item in an infant's surroundings) mediate the relationship between inner and outer reality, creating a "*potential space* between the individual and the environment" where "maximally intense experiences" are possible.[40] In this potential space, something that is experienced as an extension of the self (as continuous) can also be externalized (as contiguous), as when the mother's breast or a favored blanket or soft toy is both part of and external to a child who is nursing, or when children are experienced as both part of but external to their parents—or when fieldnotes are experienced as forging a connection between the ethnographer, ethnographic subjects, and ethnographic writing, as previously discussed.

As Adam Phillips notes in his insightful interpretation of Winnicott's approach to the therapeutic encounter, "It would sometimes seem as though for him the (perhaps unconscious) aim of any method, or set of rules, was to make possible new kinds of anomalies."[41] Winnicott's theory of potential space as a breach in the fabric of reality in which seemingly incompatible truths are experienced as real is a focal point of our analysis in chapter 4.

Lastly, our understanding of entanglement and its relevance for ethnography has been shaped by popular accounts of quantum physics, as these describe how physicists are reaching conclusions about time and space that seem like logical impossibilities from the vantage point of classical physics. In classical physics, any particle (or other object) has a well-defined position in space. By contrast, quantum objects do not exist in the same way. Just as both adoption and immigration are a kind of extreme that defies traditional understandings of location and movement by suggesting that individuals can move without fully leaving or can be in more than one location at the same time, so too will the position of a quantum object vary from experiment to experiment in a random way when measurements are performed on it—that is, the quantum object will seemingly occupy many (potential) positions at once. Perhaps more disturbing from a classical point of view is when quantum physics discusses two quantum objects: when two particles interact, they are said to have become entangled, thus losing their separate existence.[42] If they then fly apart and become separated by a great distance, a measurement on one of the particles immediately changes what we know about the other—what Einstein called "spooky action at a distance."[43] This kind of "spooky action" is reminiscent of the accounts of Swedish adoptees whose discovery of themselves in an orphanage registry in Ethiopia (see Case 2) reconfigures their experience of a postadoption reality that transformed them into "completely Swedish" persons. Just as Winnicott explores the creative potential for self-realization in "the hypothetical area that exists (but cannot exist)" at the boundaries of inner and outer reality, so too does "spooky action" provide a way of thinking about how phenomena that were once entangled but are worlds apart can move one another.[44]

In exploring ethnographic and other entanglements, we build on and contribute to recent developments in our own discipline of anthropology, such as attention to documents and reworkings of the concept of liminality. Anthropologists have studied documents in order to understand bureaucratic processes, the workings of law in practice, technologies of knowledge production, law's materiality, and the power relations that underlie both surveillance and silence.[45] We build on this work by highlighting the fantastical and emotional dimensions of documentation. To do so, we explicate the ways in which documentation is itself a form of entanglement, in that documents are external to yet inseparable from the realities to which they refer.[46] In this sense, documents serve as transitional objects between incompatible realities. In our opening vignettes, for example, the DNA test that is taken as legally compelling evidence that Ms. L. is S.S.'s mother is both external (an artificial, even alien form of measurement) and internal (constituted by and constitutive of the parent-child relationship) to Ms. L. and S.S. Likewise, the record that Sara found in the orphanage in Addis Ababa was an externalization of the self, "a part of you that you know is a part," yet when Sara found a way to relate to this externalized self, she was able to reinvent her Swedishness. The close association of documents with people makes the documents both powerful and suspect—that is, they become objects of emotional investment, something that people save, amass, or in some cases fear.[47] Some undocumented immigrants, for example, collect receipts, check stubs, and other records of their daily lives in hopes of eventually being able to regularize their status, even as such individuals often fear being discovered through the records that others keep about them.[48] Likewise, for those who are adopted, official birth certificates generated by adoption may be regarded as counterfeit—officially sanctioned documents that displace a "real" original that has been sealed or canceled so as to legitimize their rebirth in the adoptive family.[49] We further explore documentation as a form of entanglement and the emotional power of the document as a transitional object in chapter 4.[50]

We also contribute to literature by anthropologists and other scholars that has reworked notions of liminality. For example, sociologist Cecilia Menjívar productively coined the term "liminal legality" to describe the temporary and partial forms of legality that are sometimes available to migrants. As Menjívar explains, "'Liminal legality' is characterized by its ambiguity, as it is neither an undocumented status nor a documented one, but may have the characteristics of both. Importantly, a situation of 'liminal legality' is neither unidirectional nor a linear process, or even a phase from undocumented to documented status, for those who find themselves in it can return to an undocumented status when their temporary statuses end."[51] Scholars have found the concept of liminality useful to describe the indefinite waiting to which migrants are subjected as well as the ambiguity of being both yet neither.[52] Likewise, our discussion of entanglement highlights the ways that adoptees, immigrants, and exilic peoples are betwixt and between, existing in multiple worlds at the same time but also in a space that is excluded from each. Instead of implying that there are nonliminal beings, as does the concept of liminality, the concept of entanglement focuses attention on the ways that conventional accounts of the world traffic in the very forms of being that such accounts problematize.

Finally, our analysis of entanglement is indebted to work on the multiple forms of consciousness and ways of seeing that are produced when one exists on a boundary between racialized worlds. W. E. B. Du Bois, for example, writes that Black people in America experience a sense of "twoness,—an American, a Negro; two souls, two thoughts, two unreconciled strivings."[53] Relatedly, Gloria Anzaldúa defines *mestiza consciousness* as a "racial, ideological, cultural and biological cross-pollinization, an 'alien' consciousness [that] is presently in the making."[54] Transnational adoptees, unauthorized migrants, and survivors of political violence similarly exist in multiple worlds, even multiple bodies, at the same time. Recall Clara's comment, discussed in the prologue to this book, "Sometimes I forget that I am dark-skinned. When I sit with friends and chat. And then when I look in the mirror: 'Aha! That's how it is!'" As a Chilean adoptee who grew up in Sweden, Clara experienced the "alien" consciousness of being both Swedish and Chilean, two thoughts that could not be reconciled yet could not be disentangled either.

What Must Be Yet Cannot Be Real

Our analytical strategy in this book is to do the work that makes it possible to be on the interface between reality and its shadowy counterpart—that is, on the interface between what must be and what cannot be real. The Venn diagram created by artist Tucker Nichols creatively conveys this idea.

Because the realities on either side of this interface are, generally speaking, incompatible, each exerts a pull, promising a world, for example, in which it is possible to clearly differentiate between baby selling and baby making, illegal immigration and birthright citizenship, truth and fraud, experience and its representations. From within as-if worlds—whether ethnographic, legal, or so-ciological in nature—the contradictory realities that each pull sustains may be palpable; it is clear that children are potentially alienable, that citizenship and foreignness are interdependent, and that the dual location (an absent presence) occupied by ethnographers can produce insightful accounts. The analytical work that we are doing in this book is, in this sense, a type of basic research that enables us to decipher the legal forms and movements that produce belonging, alienation, membership, dislocation, home, exile, kinship, and loss.

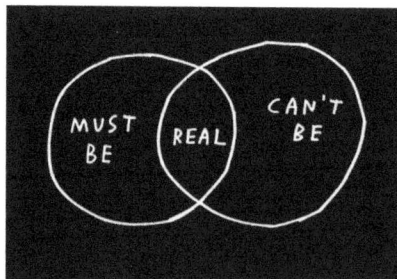

FIGURE 1.1.   Tucker Nichols, *Must Be Can't Be Real.*

A concrete example of impossible realities is provided by the following research vignette. In July 2016, Susan sat at a graffiti-covered picnic table in MacArthur Park in Los Angeles talking with Margarita (pseudonym), a Guatemalan immigrant, about her efforts to regularize her presence in the United States. Margarita had hoped to apply for deferred action—a temporary reprieve from deportation that would also grant her work authorization and the ability to get a social security number—under the Deferred Action for Parents of Americans and Lawful Permanent Residents program (commonly known as DAPA), which President Obama announced in November 2014. Margarita thought she qualified. Her two children were US citizens, and she spoke fluent English, was well educated, volunteered at her children's school, and had no criminal record. With deferred action, she and her husband would be able to launch a business, perhaps a tailor shop or floristry. However, Margarita could not apply, as a federal court had enjoined DAPA after twenty-six states, led by Texas, challenged the president's authority to create this program. The injunction had been appealed to the US Supreme Court, which, with only eight members, issued a one-sentence ruling in June 2016: "The judgment is affirmed by an equally divided Court." The lower court's injunction was allowed to stand, so DAPA did not go into effect.[55]

Unable to pursue deferred action after all, Margarita and her husband made an extraordinary decision: they revealed their undocumented status to their children. Though the children were shocked at the seeming discrepancy between the importance their parents placed on following the law and the fact that their parents had entered the country without authorization, the larger point, to Margarita, was that her children were going to have to assume responsibility for petitioning for lawful permanent residency for her and her husband when they turned twenty-one. According to Margarita, she told her oldest that he would need to petition for her husband, while her youngest would need to petition for her: "Our only hope of legalizing is through you."[56] She stressed to them that they were going to have to be financially solvent and have no criminal record in order for the petitions to succeed, so they would need to put every effort into their schooling.[57]

For Margarita, the biggest disadvantage of her undocumented status—the disadvantage that made her feel completely disoriented and out of place—was that she had become ineligible for the health care that had enabled her to survive a life-threatening disease. Even though she had been making payments to the hospital, she had recently been told that to continue to receive care, she had to purchase an insurance plan, which she could not afford. Without a work permit, she was only eligible to work at jobs where she was underpaid, the hours were long, and she was exposed to chemical-filled cleaning agents that she should have been avoiding. If she had a work permit, she explained, she would be able to afford the plan. "Me desubicó," she said, shaking her head. "I was disoriented."[58]

When asked about her plans for the future, Margarita responded, "Plans? It isn't possible to plan when you are dependent on someone else. I can dream, maybe." Her dreams were for her children to value what they had and for the United States to prosper. For herself, she wanted to do more to contribute than was possible while she lacked work authorization.

The currents swirling through this vignette illuminate the themes we introduced earlier. Margarita lives in the United States as if she is a legal resident but also as if she is not a legal resident. Her everyday life, though real, has a fictional quality, one that is continually threatened by her mode of entering the United States through a tunnel, without authorization. Though she passes as a citizen on a daily basis, she could undergo illegalization at any time, and in fact does so whenever she is asked for a work permit that she does not have. In contrast to transnational adoptees, whose parents legalize their status in the countries to which they move, Margarita has to ask her own children to legalize her status at a future date. As she discusses her daily responsibilities as a parent—walking her children to and from school because the neighborhood where she lives is dangerous—and her plan to establish her own business as a florist, the system that prohibits her presence starts to seem fantastical, imposing a needless taint of illicitness on someone whose life is very normal, a system that makes her a dependent of the politicians and judges whose actions shape her future, even though she was not part of any legal case at the time. And imposed on this discussion are the as-if conditions that are a constant backdrop of ethnographic research encounters: Who were Susan and Margarita as they participated in this exchange that made the ethnography that emerged from it possible?[59] Were we researcher and research subject, sitting at a picnic table? Two women attempting to avoid the heat while rejecting efforts of several proselytizers who tried to get us to attend a nearby prayer meeting? Two parents comparing their children's experiences learning to play musical instruments, a topic that we both seemed to enjoy discussing? What about the faith that Margarita put in the research process? When describing her concern over health care, she became emotional but declined the offer to move on to another topic, saying, "You are doing a study and you are going to publish this. So I am going to say it, even though it is painful for me. Because it is important."

This research encounter reveals both legal status and ethnographic truths to be contingent, as shown by the possibility of shifting from being an upstanding citizen to being an undocumented parent, from participating in a formal interview to being engaged in a parental conversation. Yet rather than being a falsehood or a trick, this contingency facilitates a kind of movement between realities—between (1) Margarita's sense that she should qualify for status, a reality that in many ways she already seems to have and (2) the externality that she cannot present the documentation that would allow her to work legally. Or between the moment when Margarita overcomes her emotions to speak of being turned away from the hospital that she trusted and the moment when these words are being written on this page, as part of a research account. It is through such moments and movements that ethnography creates an opening at the interface of worlds in which, to paraphrase Marilyn Strathern, both knowledges and their half-hidden counterparts—or counterfeits—are visible.[60]

At this "threshold of understanding," the contingency that is fundamental to the distinctions on which worlds are based is exposed.[61] Individuals are not intrinsically citizens, nationals, or kin; rather, they unfold as such through a series of processes. And these processes could have turned out differently, given that legal techniques "can look and turn out now one way and now another."[62] We can see this unpredictability in Margarita's experience. If President Obama's deferred action program had gone forward, she presumably would have been able to obtain a work permit and health insurance. Margarita is both akin to yet fundamentally different from a citizen. Understanding this radical (dis)similarity may make it possible to understand and interrogate the desire that countries like the United States have for both adoptable children and undocumented workers. According to the German sociologist Georg Simmel, desire has a dual significance: "It can arise only at a distance from objects, a distance that it attempts to overcome, and . . . it presupposes a closeness between the objects and ourselves in order that the distance should be experienced at all."[63] This distant closeness, in which a responsible mother who volunteers at her son's school or a child adopted by US citizens can turn out to be undocumented, may explain public fascination with and fear of adoption and immigration.

The inbetween space we seek to inhabit in this book should be familiar to ethnographers, given that ethnography, like adoption and immigration, is spatially multidimensional and temporally nonlinear. Ethnography cannot be overly instrumental, because ethnographers must become part of the fields they occupy, a position in which understanding comes in unexpected ways, as what psychologist Jerome Bruner terms "epiphanies of the ordinary," which accompany the particulars of everyday experience.[64] While others have described the dislocation that ethnography entails, we strive to attend as well to the emotional or psychological dimensions of ethnographic practices.[65] These include moments of intense experiencing in which seemingly separate people, objects, or events are felt to be connected. Ethnography hovers on a threshold, the potential space created in the as-if relationship by being immersed as a researcher in a field where people live. Immersion produces a depth of experience that takes shape in moments of separation that are also a form of connection or identification. Participant observation, the hallmark of ethnographic fieldwork, is an example of such separation that also serves as connection. Analyzing such entanglements requires following the processes of dislocation, creation, and destruction that allow the world to assume its conventional form.

Conversations

It is hard to pinpoint when we began working on this book. It might have been 1997, when Susan read Barbara's 1997 article, "Negotiating Motherhood: Identity and Difference in 'Open' Adoptions," and wrote to Barbara about the parallels between open adoption, which allowed for two sets of parents, and Mexico's decision to permit dual nationality so that Mexicans living in the United States could naturalize while retaining their Mexican legal identity. Or perhaps it was in 2000, when Barbara, Susan, and Bill Maurer spent a month at the International Institute for the Sociology of Law in Oñati, Spain, writing a paper that brought our work on transnational adoption, unauthorized immigration, and offshore finance into conversation.[66] Or it could have been in 2005, when Susan and Barbara were in Oñati again for a workshop and Susan asked Barbara and her husband, Sigfrid, what they knew about Schrödinger's cat, the name of a famous thought experiment in physics (as well as the title of a short story by Ursula K. Le Guin).[67] This question generated an in-depth conversation about particle waves, temporal paradox, the possibility of being in multiple locations at the same time, and the role of measurement in resolving irresolution. The paper that we published on these topics is also the basis for chapter 3 of this book.[68] Certainly by 2017, when we were scholars-in-residence for two weeks at the University of California Humanities Research Institute, we were working on the manuscript in earnest.

Over the course of our collaboration, we have pursued a juxtapositional or relational strategy in that we have brought together phenomena that might be presumed to be independent or distinct, creating potential space between them in which new understandings emerge. As we wrote in an earlier paper about the return trips that adoptees and deportees take to their countries of birth, "Roots trips and deportations . . . are neither intrinsically comparable nor intrinsically incomparable. Rather, juxtaposing roots trips and deportations permits particular correspondences to emerge that are both part of these two phenomena and artifacts of our own collaboration. Roots trips and deportations are rendered analogous by the relationships that juxtaposition—and our own return to our research material—brings into being."[69] Our juxtapositional strategy is intrinsically relational, as juxtapositions make it possible to discern the larger systems of which phenomena are but a part. Once this larger system comes into view, it becomes apparent that instead of being distinct, juxtaposed phenomena are entangled. For example, both transnational adoption and unauthorized migration result from the geopolitical inequalities that displace people, both adoptees and unauthorized migrants are objects of desire and fear, both those who are adopted and those who are unauthorized experience forms of social exclusion, and the very nations that practice social exclusion depend on immigrant labor and need transnational children in order to "complete" families.

We are both entangled in the phenomena that we write about, but in different ways. Since the mid-1980s, Susan has collaborated with solidarity movements that have sought justice for Central American asylum seekers and immigrants more generally, while Barbara's involvement as an adoptive parent in an open domestic adoption in the United States in the early 1980s provided an entry point for her research on policy and practice in transnational adoptions during a period of growing concern that such adoptions privileged the interests and needs of adopting parents over those of birth families. Barbara's research, which took place between 1994 and 2015, involved interviewing adoptees, adoptive parents, birth mothers, adoption agency staff, lawyers, and government officials, focusing on Sweden and the United States as adopting nations and on India, Colombia, Bolivia, Chile, Korea, and Ethiopia as sending nations. She attended workshops and conferences in South and East Asia, western Europe, and North America, at which adoption policy and practice were debated and adoption guidelines formulated, and participated in conferences organized by adult adoptees focused on racism, roots, search and reunion, and belonging. She collected government reports, news articles, and autoethnographic and documentary films, as well as memoirs, fiction, and academic theses by adult adoptees, adoptive parents, and birth mothers, all of which provide a multifaceted perspective into the ways adoption law and policy have taken shape over the course of the twentieth century and the first decade of the twenty-first, and into the experiences of those whose lives have been shaped by such law and policy.

Our account of immigration draws on Susan Coutin's 1986–2015 research regarding social, political, and legal activism on behalf of Central American immigrants and refugees. Over this period, she interviewed hundreds who had immigrated to the United States, conducted fieldwork within congregations that had declared themselves "sanctuaries" for Salvadoran and Guatemalan refugees, met with US and Salvadoran officials, observed immigration hearings in US courts, conducted life-history interviews with longtime US residents who had been deported, shadowed attorneys and paralegals as they met with clients and prepared immigration cases, attended meetings and rallies, and collected various documents, including news articles, government reports, excerpts from the *Congressional Record*, policy papers penned by Salvadoran analysts, drafts of legislation, website postings, and legal files. Together, these materials create the basis for a nuanced account of the experiences of Central American immigrants and advocates, and the legal systems within which they are situated.

We have both learned from the individuals with whom we have worked over the years, and their analyses shape our understandings. Thus, with transnational adoptees, we ask why their relationships to their birth relatives are not legally acknowledged, and with undocumented immigrants, we ask why they are often rejected as outsiders even though they typically have kin ties and lengthy periods of residence in the countries to which they move. Such questions reveal ways that the conventional world is contingent on an unconventional one whose premises defy common understandings of truth. Thus, the notion that birth establishes kin relations is connected to the possibility that all children are potentially alienable and that it is therefore law, not biology, that establishes the relationships brought into being through birth. One might imagine that adoption is an as-if relationship: a child is raised as if it were born into a given family. Yet it is defining adoptive parent-child relationships as approximations that allows those parent-child relationships that are biological to appear natural. Likewise, defining some residents as undocumented allows those who can claim citizenship to act as if they naturally belong.

We are also entangled with each other through this collaboration. Indeed, collaboration, both with each other and with our interlocutors, *is* a form of entanglement. Over our years of working together, we have developed a relationship of trust with each other. To write this book, we scheduled regular phone calls, met in person when possible, read work that each other suggested, shared detailed notes and musings, went in directions that neither of us anticipated, and came to inhabit the world with this manuscript in mind. Eventually, we reached a point where we felt that an implicit conversation was always ongoing, such that we would read a news article, hear an NPR story, go to a talk, watch a film, recall an incident, view an exhibit, or do a reading and find ourselves e-mailing each other to describe the ways that these experiences had generated some insight for our project. We followed hunches but also practiced systematic and careful documentation, drafting and exchanging notes and selecting readings that we felt would address questions that we had identified or feedback that we had received. We wrote and rewrote each chapter together, such that it is now difficult to identify passages that were written by only one of us. Our approach to writing is also informed by our engagement with undergraduate and graduate students, who are pushing faculty to reenvision research in more collaborative and politically engaged ways and to produce scholarship that is attentive to current realities.

To write this book, we have tried to envision the larger whole, within which what cannot be true also must be true and in which transnational adoption and unauthorized immigration are entangled. The genres that we juxtapose in this book have both documentary and imaginative dimensions in that they recount experiences explicitly and evocatively through analysis, narrative, visual representations, sound, and language. The accounts produced through such material, much like the subject matter of our book, are both real and not real at the same time. Memoirs are based on life experiences and are also deeply subjective; documentary films record events and histories and also represent these aesthetically; museum exhibits produce knowledge in an interactive fashion; plays may be grounded in research and are also interpreted by the director, cast, and crew in the course of their interactions over time; fiction and poetry convey truths and are also creative works; and autoethnography is systematic and constructed after the fact. In particular, we have been drawn to material that documents efforts to reconnect persons and histories across divides produced by time, distance, secrecy, and death. After assembling this collection of material, we realized that much of the work that we read or viewed addressed disappearances, a form of political violence that we also encountered in our own work on transnational adoption and unauthorized movement. Susan spent decades working with survivors of the Salvadoran civil war, and Barbara has explored the social violence that underpins the circulation of children in transnational adoption and that continues to resonate in the lives of adopted adults decades later. Through such experiences, we have witnessed how disappearing particular realities—dissidents, birth families, the ways that the United States has provoked the very migration that it officially prohibits—is also key to allowing the world to assume its conventional form. Imaginative work that records the traces of the disappeared helps us to document impossible realities that otherwise appear merely illusory, much as physicists had to engage in thought experiments in order to unsettle the underpinnings of classical physics.[70]

Memory, Entanglement, and the As If

The individual can be said to be "tangled up in stories" which happen to him before any story is recounted.

Paul Ricoeur, "Life in Quest of Narrative"

The temporal dimension is not so much about linearity, but more contiguity, not in an after from another, but in one next to the other. In this fundamental discontinuity, there are privileged moments in which occur condensations, meetings between two separate moments that come together to form a new intensity and, perhaps, enable the emergence of a true other.

J. M. Gagnebin, "On the Concept of Mimesis in the Thought of Winnicott and Benjamin"

Memory plays a key role in the imaginative work of documenting impossible realities.[71] We approach memory less as a means of recovering the past as "the way it really was" (if that is even possible) than as a process of rendering past events in light of their relation to present ones.[72] This understanding of the relationship of past to present is suggested by a conversation that Barbara had with Anna Chu-Chu Schindele, a Swedish woman who was adopted from Ethiopia, who described her return to Sweden from a trip to Addis Ababa to visit her birth family in 2005. Schindele was accompanied on the trip by her Swedish husband and her two-year-old daughter, who was introduced to her Ethiopian grandparents, aunts, uncles, and cousins for the first time. Although Schindele had visited her kin in Ethiopia several times prior to the 2005 trip, she experienced her return flight to Sweden differently on this occasion. As she explained to Barbara: "It felt like the circle was complete. It's hard to explain. It's just what I felt with my daughter on my lap. I had made this same trip when I was her age, and now I was bringing her home."[73]

While memories of events might be contrasted with imagination, which entails invention, there is a selectivity to memory, which points to the connections between imagining and remembering: both memories and imaginings develop out of perhaps infinite possibilities and are formed in relation to present realities (as in Schindele's experience).[74] As neuroscientist Lisa Feldman Barrett notes: "When your brain remembers it re-creates bits and pieces of the past and seamlessly combines them. We call this process 'remembering,' but it's really assembling. In fact, your brain may construct the same memory (or, more accurately, what you experience as the same memory) in different ways each time. . . . Every act of recognition is a construction."[75] In this sense, as Barrett argues, "Brains . . . have an amazing capacity to combine pieces of the past in novel ways. They don't merely reinstate old content: they generate new content."[76]

In this book, as we explore entanglement, we develop an account of memory in which the real makes itself felt in a moment of overlap between past and present, an overlap that brings a disappeared chapter of an individual's history to life in a "present moment," what psychologist Daniel Stern describes as "the passing moment in which something happens as the time unfolds. It is the coming into being of a new state of things, and it happens in a moment of awareness. . . . It is a small window of becoming and opportunity."[77] Drawing on Husserl's understanding of duration, Stern notes that the past of the present moment 'is still echoing at the present instant,' while the future of such a moment acts 'at the present instant to give directionality and . . . a sense of what is about to unfold.'"[78]

An example of the complexity of a "present moment" in which the past is still echoing as the future unfolds is provided in a recent talk by Stockholm psychologist Hanna Wallensteen, as part of a popular series on Sweden's Sveriges Radio,

Sommar och Vinter i P1 (Summer and winter on P1), in July 2021.[79] Wallensteen, who, like Schindele, was born in Ethiopia and adopted by Swedish parents, recalled an event that took place when she was eight years old and a new child entered her second grade class. Like Wallensteen, the new child had a familiar Swedish given name (Lisa), but unlike Wallensteen, she had an "unpronounceable" surname and a carefully styled Afro, which, according to Wallensteen, she preened self-consciously as she was introduced to the assembled children. Like Wallensteen, Lisa had "brown skin," but unlike Wallensteen, Lisa was described as "coming from Africa," a reality that rendered Wallensteen's Swedishness impossible. As she recalled that traumatic moment more than forty years previously, Wallensteen explained, "I just stood there, like an idiot, and stared at Lisa, along with the rest of the students. . . . When Lisa stepped into our world, she forced us to notice that *I, too, was 'from Africa.'*"[80] In this moment of awareness, Wallensteen's relationship to Lisa, to her classmates, and, perhaps most powerfully, to her own body—her skin, her hair, her small stature, even her "completely Swedish name"—was transformed, infecting her with a powerful unease about the meaning of "coming from Africa" and its relationship to her belonging in Sweden.[81]

Wallensteen's talk underscores both the creative potential of such moments of awareness in revisiting the past, and hints at their significance in contributing to a temporally complex process of re/membering that is a response to what Susan has described elsewhere as "dismemberment"—"processes that involve separation of persons from history, the literal injury or destruction of bodies, the embodied nature of structural violence, and the denial of membership, either by forcing people to flee their country of citizenship, by registering them in a national registry 'as if' they have no living parents, or by preventing them from being granted membership in the country where they reside."[82] Like the declaration of orphan status that made children like ChuChu and Hanna transnationally adoptable, and like the separation processes practiced at US borders that transform parent and child into deportable alien and unaccompanied minor (like Ms. L and S.S.), the erasures of dismemberment obscure the histories through which people become deportable, available for circulation in transnational adoption or disappeared physically, legally, or both from the familial or national registries that certify belonging.

Re/membering, by contrast, reassembles the past, highlighting the ways that both memory and membership are spatialized through presence, absence, and return.[83] Re/membering is temporally complex in that it suggests that memories are something to which one returns; in addition, this return may connect past and future in that revisiting the past may take place with an eye toward achieving a more just future (as in Wallensteen's case). In this sense, re/membering suggests that far from being inert, the past haunts the present. Avery Gordon defines haunting as "an animated state in which a repressed or unresolved social violence is making itself known."[84] Re/membering such unresolved social violence is a creative process, one that involves "putting life back in where only a vague memory or a bare trace was visible."[85] Re/membering is thus akin to archaeology in that it excavates the historical layers that underlie current realities, making it possible to reconnect historical conditions (such as the violence that provokes emigration or the abandonment/relinquishment of children) to what might otherwise appear to be intrinsic individual characteristics (such as illegality or adoptability). Re/membering such historical conditions is also generative in that revisiting "the conditions under which a memory was produced in the first place" makes it possible to produce "a countermemory for the future."[86] This production of a countermemory is suggested in the example of Schindele's return to Sweden with her daughter, a moment of homecoming in which continuity with the past (the seeming finality of her own departure from Ethiopia as a child) is re/membered through her daughter's homecoming to Sweden, in this way suggesting the intersection of two contiguous realities and the coming into being of a new set of relationships.

Each chapter of *Documenting Impossible Realities* examines a different facet of the intersection between what must be and cannot be real. Chapter 2 explores the binocular vision that results from bringing incompatible realities into juxtaposition. To do so, this chapter brings Gianfranco Rosi's 2016 documentary about the refugee crisis in Lampedusa into conversation with our own experiences of conducting research among the unauthorized and the transnationally adopted, as well as engaging work by other ethnographers, such as Aimee Meredith Cox and Saba Mahmood, who explore the challenges of documenting realities that are invisible.[87] In each of these examples, normality and emergency, reality and the fantastical, figure and ground, and surface and depth shift in disorienting ways. Chapter 3 examines the relationship between discovery and invention by juxtaposing physicists' accounts of the relationship between measurement and location, transnational adoptees' and US deportees' narratives about their journeys "home," and filmmaker Deann Borshay Liem's autoethnographic account of the ways that adoption produces and conceals identities. The chapter concludes with a short story that science fiction writer Ursula K. LeGuin wrote about uncertainty.[88] This material enables us to consider the role of fortuitousness and multiplicity in the construction of reality. Chapter 4 takes up the irresolution that arises when erased histories, persons, and records reassert their existence. This chapter interweaves film, autoethnography, ethnography, and memoirs of exile and political disappearances in order to examine how past and present, memory and the physical world, and even life and death are entangled. Our concluding chapter turns to quantum physics to explore how principles of nonlocality and entanglement reveal that distant and seemingly unconnected components of the universe are interrelated parts of a greater whole. Drawing on this work, we return to the as if as a relationship between interdependent yet discordant phenomena and to ethnography as a means of documenting (ir)reality.

Currents

We conclude the present chapter with a discussion of a bilingual play, *Contra la Corriente/Against the Current*, performed by the Brown Bag Theater Company at UC Irvine in May 2015 as part of the Service Workers' Project. *Contra la Corriente* can be seen as creating a potential space in which a new campus reality can be imagined. Written by Wind Woods, the play was based on interviews with UC Irvine service workers about their lives, working conditions, and struggles for justice, and was performed by drama students and some of the workers whose stories were featured in the play. *Contra la Corriente* follows several service workers as they rise in the wee hours of the morning to clean campus buildings, form friendships, are continuously under the surveillance of a boss who mistreats them, and eventually succeed in organizing a union and going on strike. In a sense, these service workers experience dislocation on their own campus in that their work often takes place outside normal business hours, when rooms and buildings are empty. The play uses the metaphor of an electrical current to describe the central yet invisible role of service workers. Against a darkened backdrop in which a single light throbs, and speaking in both English and Spanish, a narrator/labor organizer explains to the audience:

> Electricity is a powerful thing. Peligrosa. Si no está controlada. Nowadays we have found ways to control it, use it for all kinds of functions. Está alrededor de nosotros. Pulsating like, like an electric heartbeat. It courses through every inch of this building. Está aquí. En estas paredes. Underneath our feet. Y sobre nuestras cabezas. Algunos dicen que nuestro cuerpo no es nada más que electricidad.[89] There are some spaces in this world where an electric current travels between a piece of metal no thicker than a sheet of paper. Sometimes that thin sheet of metal just can't take all that energy. And it burns. Se desintegra. Disappears into nothing. La energía no puede recorrer sobre nada. When that happens, lights go out. Máquinas se detienen. Stillness.[90]

In this passage, the narrator stresses the power yet invisibility of electricity, which, he says, is in the walls, under our feet, and making up the human body. In fact, it becomes most visible in its disappearance; when a fuse blows, lights go out, machines stop, and there is nothing but stillness.[91] Current, the narrator stresses, is dangerous if not controlled.[92]

In another passage later in the play, the narrator, again speaking in both English and Spanish, reflects on the ways that workers experience campus buildings:

> Hay cientos de edificios en esta Universidad. In each room, there are corners. El lugar en donde dos paredes se unen. Corners are often the place where the most amount of dirt gathers. Muchos no se fijen en las esquinas. Most don't pay attention to the nooks and crannies of a building. But the workers understand that the most important places to clean are corners, the small space where two walls meet. There are thousands of them hidden in plain sight. Like those thoughts that everyone has but won't say.[93]

Most people—presumably the professors, students, and staff who use offices and classrooms on a daily basis—do not pay attention to the corners of rooms, because they do not have to clean them. These obscure spots are "hidden in plain sight," much like the workers themselves.[94] But to the workers, the corners may be the most important part of a building, demonstrating that space itself takes multiple forms.

Finally, toward the end of the play, a worker who has been urging her coworkers to join in a strike brings these images together, exclaiming, "¡Los trabajadores tienen el poder! Don't you see? Nosotros somos la corriente que hace funcionar esta máquina." [The workers have the power! Don't you see? We are the current that makes this machine function.] The current mentioned in the play's title, then, refers not only to electrical current but to the workers themselves, who were perhaps invisible, working in the dark, and yet without whom the campus could not function. Professors, students, and service workers were thus entangled in the ongoing work of the campus. By crossing boundaries between academia and service workers, Spanish and English, and fiction and documentation, this play created a potential space in which it was possible to see a new vision of the campus fueled by a current of service workers who dusted offices, swept floors, picked up trash, and cleaned corners. These workers have become even more important as COVID-19 led to campus closures and increased sanitation efforts.[95]

The production of impossible realities, such as those in this play, is laden with emotions. Unconventional worlds (the underground, the world people occupy *before* migrating or being adopted) fascinate, both drawing in and repelling their inhabitants. Powerful emotional connections to repressed or prohibited worlds can overwhelm those who move, leading to a sense of loss, grief, and terror. But such connections can also lead to revelations by making visible differences that are otherwise denied or hidden. Ethnographers have often struggled to understand and convey the emotional content of fieldwork experiences, while law is supposed to be dispassionate in the administration of justice. Emotions, in a sense, lie outside that which can be documented, measured, or understood but are nonetheless critical to the dislocations that we explore in this book.

FIELDSIGHT
Multivalent Ways of Seeing
in Ethnography and Law

> The perspective we need to acquire . . . has to do with a fluid
> positioning that sees back and forth across boundary, which
> acknowledges that I can be black and good and black and bad and
> that I can also be black and white, male and female, yin and yang,
> love and hate.
>
> Patricia J. Williams, *The Alchemy of Race and Rights*

In this quote, law professor and critical race theorist Patricia Williams pushes back against societal stereotypes that pin Black individuality "to the underside of this society and keep us there, out of sight/out of mind, out of the knowledge of mind which is law."[1] Instead, she advocates a "fluid positioning" that refuses essentialized binaries altogether and makes possible an "ambivalent, multivalent way of seeing."[2] To us, Williams's critique of law resonates with critiques of ethnography, while her multivalent approach evokes ethnography's potential. On the one hand, ethnography is implicated in the production of exoticized and orientalist images of racialized others, such as those that Williams challenges.[3] As indigenous studies scholar Linda Tuhiwai Smith notes, "Both the formal scholarly pursuits of knowledge and the informal, imaginative, anecdotal constructions of the Other are intertwined with each other and with the activity of research."[4] On the other hand, at its best, ethnographic fieldwork strives for fluid positioning, such as being an insider and an outsider at the same time, allowing for "see[ing] back and forth across boundary," as stated in the quote that opens this chapter. Such "seeing . . . across boundary" documents impossible realities by putting disparate or incompatible experiences into relationship with each other, thus bringing new fields into being.

To theorize how ethnographic fields of vision are created and disrupted, we draw on examples of fieldwork in both film and ethnography. We argue that fields are not simply geographical locations to which ethnographers travel in space and time (though many fields can be located in geographic space) but also as-if phenomena or transitional objects in that they are both internal to and external from ethnographers.[5] These phenomena or objects are constantly in the process of fabrication and revision as the impressions and understandings of ethnographers are transformed through multiple experiences in both the field and the academy, exchanges over time with interlocutors, engagement with other scholarly work, and conversations or collaborations with colleagues. The field is, in this sense, neither completely separable from ethnographers or the subjects of their research, nor simply a product of the ethnographic imagination.[6] Rather, like fieldnotes, fields are actualized through interaction between ethnographers, interlocutors, and ethnographic writing, creating a "potential space" that is central to the production of ethnographic knowledge.[7] Producing this potential space is a creative and collaborative process and, like other forms of research, "is not an innocent or distant academic exercise but an activity that has something at stake and that occurs in a set of political and social conditions."[8]

The juxtapositions, displacements, and movements that create fields locate filmmakers, ethnographers, and others on the threshold between worlds, at least temporarily. We refer to the mode of perception enabled by such positioning as fieldsight. By exploring the nature of fieldsight, we seek to push the boundaries of field sciences such as anthropology, botany, and geology into new territory. Traditionally, anthropology and related field sciences presumed that fields existed prior to the arrival of researchers, who were generally not part of the communities being studied and who traveled there in order to encounter phenomena, record data, and gather samples.[9] Early ethnographers, for example, participated in expeditions as naturalists, who were as interested in zoology, geography, and geology as in ethnology.[10] Even today, anthropologists say things like, "Next year, I will be in the field," as though it is clear where or what that might be. Such a statement implies interchangeability between the field as a geographical location, set of activities, stage of research, or even stage of ethnographers' own development (as when students go through the phase of being "in the field").[11] Thus, the field is as much a state of being and a condition of the ethnographer as it is a specific place, social phenomenon, or context. Moreover, critiques of the fraught and often unequal relationship between researchers and subjects have led to a proliferation of potential field sites as well as a broader range of people—notably those who have conventionally been the subjects of ethnographic study—becoming ethnographers. Ethnographers have been urged to "study up" and to conduct research "at home," within their own institutions and communities.[12] As a result, the domain that can be constituted as a field is now almost unbounded, and travel is no longer necessarily required. Yet distance, at least of the emotional variety, is another matter. As Cerwonka and Malkki point out, ethnographers are often asked whether they are too close to their research but are rarely asked if they are "close enough," and those who carry out research within their own communities must navigate a complex set of relationships.[13] More generally, even though ethnographers are often admonished to maintain a certain distance from their subject matter, fieldwork, as we noted in chapter 1, is also supposed to proceed through immersion—that is, entering and remaining fully in the field for a lengthy period of time, such that the distinction between researcher and site gradually diminishes.

The proliferation yet instability of ethnographic fields suggests that the relationship between ethnographers' presence and the spaces in which fieldwork occurs is spatially and temporally complex. There is a sense in which presence—and its counterpart, absence—brings space into being.[14] Thus, a particular location, set of social relationships, or type of activity becomes a field (or potential field) in the ethnographic sense through the entanglement of ethnographers and interlocutors. Fields can thus materialize and disappear, even as they have histories that also accompany their instantiation. Fields therefore have a dual quality: they are there and not there at the same time, potentially situating the ethnographer in the nowhere of a breach or gap between worlds. This positioning, in a breach or gap, can make ethnography a fraught experience.

Fire at Sea

> I have to grab and grasp the truth that belongs so intimately to each of [the characters] and a little fragment of life—their life. That is the truth in the documentary. I am not talking about the difference between fiction and non-fiction documentary. The truth is what it is. And it's their truth, it is their moment—a portrait of them.
>
> Filmmaker Gianfranco Rosi quoted in a 2014
> interview with Frank Ombres

Filmmaker Gianfranco Rosi's documentary *Fire at Sea* (*Fuocoammare*) provides an example of the process of actualizing an ethnographic field. *Fire at Sea* examines the refugee crisis that unfolded in the sea surrounding the Italian island of Lampedusa, beginning in the late 1990s and continuing into the 2000s. The film begins by displaying statistics: Lampedusa is 70 miles from Tunisia and 120 miles from Sicily—closer to Africa than to the rest of Italy—and fifteen thousand people have died trying to cross the Mediterranean to get there. After presenting these sobering facts, the filmmaker assembles a montage of moments from daily life in Lampedusa, without narration, music, plot, or explanation. Some moments are harrowing and difficult to watch, while others are mundane in their ordinariness. An opening scene depicts a young boy trying to climb a tree. Is this one of the refugees? Is he trying to look out into the sea, perhaps for a ship? As the boy continues struggling to gain a foothold, the viewer can hear twigs breaking and a low murmur as the boy talks to himself. Gradually, viewers may realize that the boy is Italian. He finally clambers up, breaks off a branch, and begins to whittle it. Perhaps he is simply playing. On the surface, this scene seems to have nothing to do with the journeys and deaths mentioned at the outset. As the film continues, though, it becomes clear that the boy and the refugees inhabit the same field: the sea, the island, the doctor's office—and it is the work of the filmmaker that makes this field apparent. As one film critic observed, "Rosi's game is to bring the migrants and their plight gradually closer."[15]

The strategies that Rosi uses to produce this and other documentaries bear striking resemblance to ethnographic practices. Rosi told journalist Franco Ombres, "I start with an encounter with a place."[16] Indeed, Rosi lingers in the moments that he films: a woman named Maria making up a bed, a migrant crying inconsolably, a diver shining his searchlight underwater as he gathers octopus from an underwater trap, the seemingly endless reach of the ocean as a spotlight scans the surface, the search for a missing boat that was carrying migrants. Rosi deliberately attempts to disrupt more typical narratives of documentaries: "In many documentaries there's always this complaining and explaining, or explaining and complaining. . . . So in my film nobody complains about their situation. I don't want you to know it, and I wouldn't try to solve it. It's quite intentional."[17] Though Rosi does not try to explain, he does pursue truth: "It is still a documentary because everything I filmed is absolutely true."[18] And the truth that Rosi strives for sounds very ethnographic: "It's about showing a certain kind of people. And somehow these people are able to express larger society in a different way, and that's what fascinates me."[19] Yet accurately depicting this truth involves transformation, as the place in which Rosi lingers becomes "an abstraction. . . . The place has been transformed" into an unrecognizable place, what one might call a field.[20]

The field explored in *Fire at Sea* has depths and surfaces, presences and absences, and disorienting juxtapositions. In an early scene, a searchlight sweeps across the moving surface of the water while voices are heard repeating, "Please, we beg you, we are sinking," and a radio operator asks over and over, "Your position? Your position?" The disembodied voices (Was their boat found?) draw attention to the death that lies beneath the surface, perhaps not only beneath the surface of the sea but beneath life in Lampedusa as well. In fact, in another scene, a doctor describes the hold of a boat, where those who pay the least crowd in and become the first to drown or suffocate as water enters and air becomes scarce. From the outside, one can never tell, he says, how many people are in the boat. The skin is another surface, one that burns when it is exposed to leaking fuel on the boat, which could, as a rescue worker comments, burst into flames if there was a spark. Fluids also lie beneath the skin, as we see when the doctor examines a refugee woman who is pregnant with twins. Her babies are intertwined, making it hard to determine their sex; the entangled babies in scarce amniotic fluid are a seeming metaphor for the difficulties of the refugees who are entangled with Lampedusa but who perhaps are not seen either. History also lies below the surface of daily life, as the Italian boy, whose name, we learn, is Samuele, listens to his grandmother tell stories of the fire at sea that occurred during wartime, when navy ships passed at night. The film's title is also a song that a DJ plays to honor fishermen who cannot go out due to stormy weather. The DJ is an enigmatic character who seems to have no connection to the refugees; perhaps he is something of a present absence within the film, channeling the emotions of Lampedusa residents through their requests for songs like "Fuocoammare."

As the film moves between Samuele's daily life and that of the refugees who risk drowning, suffer dehydration, sing of their travails, and play soccer, background and foreground continually shift, disorienting the viewer, perhaps as both Lampedusans and refugees are themselves disoriented. For example, as one critic remarked, "Samuele is the opposite of a point-of-view character. We see what he doesn't."[21] The disparate realities of Samuele doing his English homework and a man struggling to breathe as his limp body is carried onto a rescue ship suggest that the refugees have become something of a routine exception in that their arrival is now part of life on the island. And throughout the film, both we, and the boy Samuele, learn to see. Samuele, it turns out, has lazy eye, so he does not succeed in hitting birds with the slingshot that he fashioned from the branch in the first scene. After the doctor prescribes a patch, his vision improves, and toward the end of the film, he sees a bird, but instead of trying to kill it, he caresses its head. Perhaps it is only when he sees the baby bird properly that he is able to have compassion for it, but seeing it properly was contingent on using a patch, which temporarily obscured his vision.

Likewise, for Rosi, insights are made possible through the pretense of being elsewhere. He explains, "I was born in Africa. I lived in Turkey, I moved to New York and stayed there for many years. I have a double nationality. And even when I shot in Rome, it was like being somewhere else. I like the idea of being somewhere else."[22] Perhaps the illusion of being transported elsewhere is what makes it possible to see, much like ethnographers may strive to maintain a degree of distance when joining in social interactions. Indeed, such juxtapositions of perspective create what literary anthropologist Wolfgang Iser refers to as "manifold mirrorings." Iser writes, "In Nietzsche's terms: 'If we try to observe the mirror in itself, we finally discover nothing but things on it. If we want to grasp the things, we ultimately come upon nothing other than the mirror.'"[23] A scene from *Fire at Sea* that similarly destabilizes the distinctions between reality, observation, and reflection takes place at night, inside a rescue ship, where a helicopter that is out on the deck, preparing to depart, can be seen on a monitor. When the helicopter takes off, it disappears from the monitor, only to reappear through the ship's window. Jarringly, seeing the helicopter through the window reveals that the earlier view on the monitor was not "real" but mediated by a security camera. But of course the view through the window was not "real" either, as it appeared on the screen on which *Fire at Sea* played.

Fieldwork, much like Gianfranco Rosi's filmmaking in Lampedusa, requires undoing the very boundaries on which fields depend. There are disjunctures between ongoing social life and its shadowy or as-if counterpart, which is the field brought into being through ethnographic fieldwork, an activity that, if it is to have meaning, can never consist only of research. Ethnographers occupy both of these versions of reality (i.e., ongoing social life and the ethnographic field), thus existing on multiple planes and in the breach between them, much like Lampedusa is both a place of death and the place where Samuele has English class. Unlike the notion that ethnographers must maintain distance, which implies that proximity is a continuum, disjuncture suggests that there is a multiplicity of realities, a multiplicity that cannot be reduced to cultural differences between ethnographer and interlocutors. Occupying the gap or breach between field and not-field gives ethnographers a sort of double vision, perhaps akin to what Rosi describes as "a mental space, which is somehow the border—there's an empty space that I have to fill with stories. So there's always an encounter with a place, *and then that place becomes a mental space.* . . . Basically it's a real place that has to be transformed."[24] Such transformations, along with the complex relations between field and not-field that they set in motion, make fieldsight possible.

The Wonder of Appearance

> For [Benjamin] the size of an object was in an inverse ratio to its significance. . . .
> The smaller the object, the more likely it seemed that it could contain in the most concentrated form everything else. . . . And this paradox—or, more simply, the wonder of appearance—was always at the center of his concerns.
> Arendt, introduction to Walter Benjamin's *Illuminations*

Our understanding of fieldsight is indebted to Gregory Bateson's exploration of binocular (or stereoscopic) vision as providing "an extra *dimension* to seeing" in the form of an image "which appears to be undivided, [but] is in fact a complex synthesis of information . . . from which all traces of the vertical boundary have disappeared."[25] Bateson argues that this kind of double vision and the complex synthesis of information it makes possible "*is* the relationship" (emphasis in original)—including the relationship of ethnographers to their interlocutors—and provides an understanding of contextual learning "that is different from what the experimenters see."[26] Bateson illustrates the depth provided by binocular vision with material from *Naven*, his ethnography of gender dynamics among the Iatmul of Papua New Guinea, likening the ethnographer's dependence on a double (or relational) perspective for learning the contexts of life in an unfamiliar cultural environment to a similar dialectical process through which gendered and other aesthetic forms take shape in everyday and ceremonial interactions among the people being studied.[27] In each case, both gender (as practiced and experienced by the Iatmul) and claims to discovering the truth about Iatmul gender (as practiced and experienced by the ethnographer) are contingent on an imaginative act of mirroring and invention. Such an act can take shape only in the gap or breach between, as Rosi put it, "an encounter with a place" [with a person] and the transformation of that place [that person] into "a mental space . . . that I have to fill with stories."[28]

Like Bateson and Rosi, D. W. Winnicott—known for his contributions to object relations theory and specifically for his clinical research on the developing child's engagement with the world of shared reality—is attentive to the key role of the interplay between the internal and the external in creating this shared world. Moving away from conventional understandings of the individual as "a unit with a limiting membrane and an outside and an inside," Winnicott noted that his clinical practice "attempt[ed] to get in between these two extremes," to a more complex analysis of "an intermediate area of *experiencing* to which inner reality and external life both contribute."[29] Winnicott described this intermediate area of experiencing as a potential space that takes shape between mother and infant, a space characterized by "remembering, reliving, fantasying, dreaming . . . [and] the integrating of past, present, and future."[30]

To capture the precariousness of this ephemeral location, Winnicott developed the concept of a "continuity-contiguity moment" and suggested that "the verbal noun 'playing'" best captures the forms of interaction that are catalyzed there.[31] As Marie Claire Sekkel notes in her insightful exploration of the moment where continuity gives way to contiguity: "The sense of continuity is achieved through the perception of contiguous situations (close and separate), made possible by the relationships of similarity, that link worlds. . . . The blanket which has the mother's smell, for example, acquires value for the baby not just because of the smell, but due to the power of bringing to oneself the world the mother inhabits, and, along with it, the sense of continuity of being. The blanket/transitional object is the child's creation in which a flash of otherness was condensed into a blanket/object."[32]

Just as the child's blanket becomes a condensation of a "flash of otherness" for the child, even as it is used by the child to invent/discover its continuity of being with the mother, so too does Bateson's concept of binocular vision, with its two-eyed method of seeing, provide a metaphor for the way "we *draw* distinctions; that is, we *pull* them out" of events "that correspond to *outlines* in the visible world. . . . Those distinctions that remain undrawn are *not*" (emphases in original).[33] In this sense, "Difference, being of the nature of relationship, is not located in time or space. . . . *Difference does not have a location*."[34] Rather, difference is present as what literary anthropologist Wolfgang Iser terms "an existent 'nonreality.'"[35] An example of such an existent nonreality is an intense experience of connection that Winnicott likens to electricity when used to capture intimate or meaningful contact, as when people are in love.[36]

The notion that binocular vision generates insights also resonates with the Chicana cultural theorist Gloria Anzaldúa's concept of mestiza consciousness. According to Anzaldúa, "Racial, ideological, cultural and biological cross-pollinization" associated with borderlands produces multiple perspectives that are also shaped by power relations, giving rise to an "'alien' consciousness . . . presently in the making."[37] Significantly, this "alien" consciousness is internal and external at the same time, as Cantú and Hurtado explain:

> Anzaldúa asserts, living the borderlands produces knowledge by being within a system while also retaining the knowledge of an outsider who comes from outside the system. This "outsider within" status gives Chicanas' sense of self a layered complexity that is captured in Anzaldúa's concept of mestiza consciousness. . . . Their ability to "see" the arbitrary nature of all social categories but still take a stand challenges Chicana feminisms to exclude while including, to reject while accepting, and to struggle while negotiating. The basic concept involves the ability to hold multiple social perspectives while simultaneously maintaining a center that revolves around fighting against concrete material forms of oppression.[38]

Through such "layered complexity," those with a mestiza consciousness are able to grasp impossible realities created by systems of oppression that define people who are within a system as outsiders who do not belong. Significantly, Anzaldúa applied this notion of mestiza consciousness not only to Chicanas but also to those who cross political, sexual, and social borders. Rather than being a static form of being, such consciousness is dynamic and in the making.

Transnational adoptees and immigrants, who often describe being in yet excluded from multiple places at the same time, are gifted with a kind of double vision, perhaps akin to what W. E. B. Du Bois describes as second sight: "It is a peculiar sensation, this double-consciousness, this sense of always looking at one's self through the eyes of others, of measuring one's soul by the tape of a world that looks on in amused contempt and pity. One ever feels this twoness."[39] Sofia Berzelius—who was born in Ethiopia, adopted by Swedish parents when she was an infant, and raised in Sweden, where media coverage of Ethiopia presented that country primarily in imagery of starvation and death—provides an example of feeling this "twoness." Longing to find out what the country she was identified with by others was really like—another adoptee described it as "that irritating Ethiopianness" that was a constant presence in her life in Sweden—Sofia traveled to Addis Ababa as an adult in hopes of finding files relating to her adoption and of visiting the hospital where she was born. In Sweden, she had been told the hospital no longer existed and that there were no records of her birth family, but in Addis Ababa, she found both. Upon arriving at the hospital that was "actually being rebuilt at the moment when we were there," she recalls thinking, "This is so crazy. We have just been at the place where I found files relating to my birth mother, and it is maybe an hour later and we are standing here in this hospital that doesn't even exist!"

On her return to Sweden, Sofia was intensely aware of the reality of an Ethiopia that had been closed to her since her adoption, explaining how unfathomable it was to her "that this life in Ethiopia carries on when I am not there. In this very moment, they are still there and they are still walking there and they are still breathing that air and they are still eating that delicious food and they are still starving. And I go back here and I just—I mean, drinking tap water, what a crazy thing to do." Her simultaneous connection to and quasi-presence in two places redefines her understanding of everyday objects, such as tap water, which is risky to drink in Ethiopia but commonly consumed in Sweden. At the same time, as Sofia explained,

> I have never taken [these things] for granted, I have always been thinking, "This is such a privilege. This is such a privilege." It has been obvious to me that this is not something that everybody does. I guess it's something, maybe it's just very simple identification and you are four years old and you watch TV and you see people that look the same way as you do and they carry their water. I guess something happened in my four-year-old mind. Therefore I've never taken it for granted. And then it was this thing, this feeling that I should be grateful to be here. Of course, I have everything here, so why am I not completely happy? It's confusing.[40]

These moments of intense experiencing, when the self takes shape vis-á-vis a canceled Other, "link the past, the present, and the future; *they take up time and space.* They demand and get our concentrated deliberate attention, deliberate but without too much of the deliberateness of trying" (emphasis in original).[41] Winnicott conceptualizes such moments and the experiences they provoke as processes of "reality testing" in an intermediate zone "between what is objectively perceived and what is subjectively conceived of."[42] This intermediate zone is emotionally intense in that it involves both "the *illusion* that there is an external reality that corresponds to [the individual's] own capacity to create" and disillusionment (or intense fear) that a desired (but impossible) reality will fully materialize (emphasis in original).[43] In Sofia's retelling, she describes her discovery of the hospital that does not even exist as "crazy" and "this fantastic thing [that] happens." But she also recounted her fear when she boarded the flight that would return her to Ethiopia for the first time: "I was so frightened, I was very, very scared, I really haven't liked traveling ever. I just had this feeling that I would never, ever come back to Sweden. . . . And then when the plane lifted from the ground, I was sort of sad. I thought, 'This is stupid, I shouldn't do this. I am too young; I will never return. I like my parents. So it was strange."

In a second example of double consciousness, Kanthi Grünewald, who was born in Kolkata, India, returned with her adoptive mother, Annika, to visit the orphanage where Kanthi had spent the first four years of her life. In an article written for an adoptive parent journal, Annika described Kanthi's desire to return to India, even as she noted her fear of meeting children who "didn't even have an orphanage to be in."[44] At the orphanage, they saw children who sat with crossed legs and did nothing, one of them developmentally disabled. Her mother observed that Kanthi "once sat just in that place." That evening in their hotel room, Kanthi, who was ten years old, said to her mother, "Imagine if I had been left there and you had adopted another child and you had come back with her and were looking at me."[45] In this powerful moment, Kanthi situated her self both inside and outside the orphanage. She was simultaneously the orphanage child (the child who sat with crossed legs and did nothing) and the Swedish child, Kanthi, who could gaze at this child because of a chance encounter that took her to Sweden. Her capacity to experience her exchangeability with the orphanage child and the transactional nature of the adoption process reflects the double vision she acquired as an adoptee, who had lived for almost half her life in an orphanage in India before being adopted by a family in Sweden. Was she Indian? Swedish? Could she fully belong to her adopted family if she had an orphanage family in Kolkata? And what was her connection to this orphanage (family) that went on being after she went away?[46]

Like these adoptees, immigrants to the United States described existing in multiple yet incompatible worlds. During a 2001 interview with Susan, Katarina Martínez, who had immigrated to the United States without authorization as a young child during the Salvadoran civil war, explained her complicated legal situation:

> There are always constant reminders that I'm not supposed to be here. . . . Like, going to university, looking at the applications. Well, I can't say that I'm a resident, and I can't say that I'm not a resident. And then, I have no memory [of El Salvador]. . . . Thinking of going back is so terrifying to me, because I don't know that place. . . . As long as my family is with me I have a home, you know? But other than that, it's like there is nothing. There is nothing here, there is nothing there, it's a strange situation to be in. . . . Talking to people I have no, it's like, for a minute you have no identity outside of your house. That's what it feels like sometimes. You're just walking around, and you're just, you're like invisible to everything else. Everybody else is solid but you're not. It just happens to me once in a while.

In this passage, Katarina describes the multiple worlds that she occupies. Unlike Sofia Berzelius, whose return trip to Ethiopia enabled her to see life in Ethiopia in vivid detail even when she was away in Sweden, Katarina's double vision is of a void, the nothingness of her life in the United States, where she lacked permanent status, and the nothingness of her potential future should she be deported to El Salvador, of which she had no memory. Her complex position as neither a resident nor a nonresident—at the time of our interview, she had a pending application for US residency under the Nicaraguan Adjustment and Central American Relief Act—allowed her to perceive reality differently. She could see that others were solid (presumably firmly planted in the United States) while she was not, perhaps due to occupying multiple places, including a void, at the same time. Outside her own home, she felt that she had no identity and became invisible, unable to vote, register as a university student, or reminisce about her childhood in El Salvador, as though she had no history.

Likewise, Diana, who had immigrated to the United States from Mexico without authorization as a seventeen-year-old in 1994, had developed a complex understanding of the relationship among space, presence, and illegality.[47] Despite—or perhaps because of—being undocumented, Diana had attempted to organize other undocumented women. During a 2015 interview with Gray Abarca, who was collaborating with Susan in carrying out research, Diana described the challenges these women faced:

> No one, as I tell you, no one [goes] around saying they are undocumented. No one speaks of that, because of the shame of "Invisible! Invisible!" No? . . . I see that there is great isolation in the community, as I see

in the women, some women who are in their homes, who work at home, who do not have a job in which someone pays them, they don't have a way to show how much time they have here in this country. Plain and simple, invisible people. Totally invisible. They are here in downtown Los Angeles but they are in a hole under the ground, do you understand me?

Diana is able to see that undocumented women are both in the center of Los Angeles and in a hole underground, a reflection of the way that they are simultaneously present, working in homes, but absent, because their lives do not produce the sort of documentation (such as check stubs) that would enable them to regularize their status if the opportunity arose. Central yet isolated, these women, like Diana herself, occupy multiple realities.

While undocumented immigrants, transnational adoptees, ethnographers, and filmmakers are positioned very differently, enjoying privilege in some cases and facing marginalization in others, juxtaposing their experiences suggests that constructing or forcing some people to occupy as-if fields helps to define the worlds of nation-states, scientific knowledge, and other families as conventional. For the undocumented, illegality can materialize suddenly—when filling out an application to attend college or when seeking proof of presence. Individuals are not intrinsically illegal; rather, they are constructed as such through practices (demanding documentation, denying work opportunities) that displace them from the worlds that others occupy, positioning them in a domain of illegality. In addition, adoptees' kin relations are both produced and undone through acts of severance and of joining that inseparably link a form of outlaw time (a period when they have been declared to be "legal orphans" or "legally abandoned" beings, even though they have biological parents) to legal transactions. It was such an illegal moment that Kanthi experienced when she returned to the orphanage in Kolkata and saw herself in the child left behind in the orphanage.[48] Immigrants and adoptees are forced to inhabit worlds that are simultaneously legal and illegal, natural and constructed, solid and a void. Their descriptions of these experiences reveal the as-if quality of worlds that, to nonimmigrants and nonadoptees, may seem complete and unproblematic, worlds in which biological ties are of course the basis for kinship and territorial borders of course define the grounds of belonging. Revealing these as-if qualities denaturalizes these taken-for-granted worlds, bringing out dimensions of being that were there all along.[49]

Sofia's, Kanthi's, Katarina's, and Diana's accounts of occupying the breach between these worlds are examples of the condensations between seemingly separate moments that we previously described.[50] In such moments of similarity, visible and invisible worlds merge, disrupting fictions of the radical difference between the orphanage child who belongs in India and the adopted one who is completely Swedish, or related fictions about the integrity of borders between the United States and Mexico. In fact, such disruptions—and the condensations or new intensities they create—have implications for the ways through which institutions of kinship, citizenship, and belonging are configured.[51]

Shapeshifting

> Shapeshifting is an act, a theory, and, in this sense, a form of praxis that . . . reveals our collective vulnerabilities.
>
> Aimee Cox, *Shapeshifters: Black Girls and the Choreography of Citizenship*

In her ethnography of a Detroit shelter for young women and girls, most of whom are Black, anthropologist Aimee Cox develops the notion of "shapeshifting" to describe the ways that shelter residents' analyses and embodied practices reenvision the institutions that allegedly help so-called at-risk youth overcome obstacles and progress socially. These institutions—schools, shelters, nonprofits—begin with the premise that young Black girls are a problem, that they suffer from pathologies of various sorts, and that with proper guidance and discipline they can achieve respectability in the form of employment, law abidingness, and stable family relationships. As do her interlocutors, Cox rejects "the limited social scripts they are allowed to live and speak from" to instead focus on Black girls' own narratives and practices.[52] These girls shapeshift—that is, they perform "cultural work" by "mobiliz[ing] history, whether officially documented or bricolaged through recall and desire, to give new meaning to social contexts that engender cartographic capacities beyond particular physical or ideological sites."[53] For example, during her fieldwork, Cox became close to a multigenerational Black family she calls the Browns, two members of whom—Janice and Crystal—moved in and out of the shelter. The Browns' experiences in some ways epitomize broader narratives about risk, deviancy, and danger. Not all family members were employed, and some worked at low-wage jobs, discontinued their educations, or became parents at a young age. Yet Janice's and Crystal's accounts of their family history reject such pathologizing characterizations to instead emphasize the ways that family members have practiced an ethic of care despite not being granted the rights and material conditions that would enable them to thrive. Through these accounts, Janice and Crystal produce "a shift in the shape of the city."[54] This shift maps how "the process of showing care in relationships should extend . . . from spaces we categorize as either private or public, and from social actors we are bound to, through an interconnected web of entitled care. It must also include the right to participate in the processes of citizenship—even as young Black women like Janice question its inequitable terms."[55]

Shapeshifting is a form of fieldsight in that it entails constructing visions of reality that transcend visible and invisible worlds. To transcend such worlds, both the shelter residents and Cox herself take into account the all-too-often hidden inequities that underlie what are otherwise construed as pathologies or problems. Cox points out that "Black girls and young women living in or close to poverty are the population most adversely affected by the implementation of these laws and reforms [e.g., policies restricting reproductive rights or reducing unemployment assistance]. Their vulnerabilities, however, are concealed by their displacement from the dialogues that swirl around them, even as these dialogues are grounded (on all sides of the debate) on intractable assumptions about Blackness, youth, gender, sexuality, and class."[56] Yet though they are displaced from debates, Black women and girls are "fully centered in their own lives and their communities."[57] This combination of displacement and centering produces the kind of double vision that is central to fieldsight. For example, shelter residents developed a project that they called the Move Experiment. Residents worked with Cox—who was a dancer and choreographer in addition to being an anthropologist—to study dance and to perform their own pieces. This project eventually became a form of improvisational political theater. Participants performed at places like bus stops, and after a crowd gathered, they would freeze; ask an onlooker to pull a quote, poem, or statement out of a hat; read it aloud; and then have an impromptu discussion. They would then resume their performance. This innovative outreach strategy enabled participants to share their insights, "mov[ing] from a place of intuitive knowing" that both was grounded in and transcended experience.[58]

As an ethnographer, Cox joined in these activities, carrying out "coperformative witnessing"—a form of participant observation that required establishing enduring connections and relationships as well as engaging in the material and political conditions of others.[59] Cox treated her interlocutors' insights as theory, drawing on their concepts as well as on academic literature to make sense of the ethnographic material. One such concept was entitlement. As Cox explains, "Entitlement as theorized by Janice—the central figure in this ethnography—and the other young Black women in this book . . . is an empowered statement that disputes the idea that only certain people are worthy of the rights of citizenship and the ability to direct the course of their lives."[60] Such concepts and the visions that they reference help to bring readers into the fields that Cox and her interlocutors inhabit, enabling a sort of shapeshifting among ethnographers, ethnographic writing, and ethnographic subjects, as though a common current runs through them all.

The sort of deep engagement entailed in shapeshifting requires moving between conflicting accounts, keeping both alive at the same time, and is thus key
to documenting impossible realities. Patricia Williams accomplishes this sort of
movement in her book *The Alchemy of Race and Rights*.[61] Throughout the book,
Williams juxtaposes standard definitions of law as clear, transcendent, and
objective with accounts of her own experiences, including her encounters with
and analyses of news events.[62] Williams describes her strategy as follows:

> This sort of analytic technique can serve to describe a community of
> context for those social actors whose traditional legal status has been the
> isolation of oxymoron, of oddity, of outsider. I am trying to create a
> genre of legal writing to fill the gaps of traditional legal scholarship.
> I would like to write in a way that reveals the intersubjectivity of legal
> constructions, that forces the reader both to participate in the construc-
> tion of meaning and to be conscious of that process. . . . I hope that the
> gaps in my own writing will be self-consciously filled by the reader, as
> an act of forced mirroring of meaning-invention. To this end, I exploit
> all sorts of literary devices, including parody, parable, and poetry.[63]

By bringing the experiences of law's Others into view, Williams demonstrates the
sleight of hand through which standard legal arguments about affirmative action,
crime, and personal responsibility ignore social inequality even as they treat efforts to redress inequality as unfair. She points out, for example, that formal equality is empty if not accompanied by recognition of historical inequities, that
projecting criminality onto Black Americans turns attention away from white
criminality, and that destitute mothers are held legally accountable for being poor
even though there is no legal requirement for governments to provide mothers
with a means of livelihood.

In disrupting law's presumed universality through outsider storytelling, Williams deploys a form of fieldsight that resonates with our earlier discussion of binocular vision. Williams tells a story about how on a family trip when they were
kids, she and her sister argued about the color of the highway. She saw the highway
as black, and her sister saw it as purple. After endless fighting, her sister finally
agreed that it was black, but Williams's father pointed out that no matter what her
sister said, she actually saw purple. Williams learned that "it really is possible to
see things—even the most concrete things—simultaneously yet differently; and
that seeing simultaneously yet differently is more easily done by two people than
one, but that one person can get the hang of it with time and effort."[64] That which
is seen "simultaneously yet differently" takes multiple forms. Thus, legal rights are
both stable and unstable, insufficient yet key: "To say that blacks never fully believed in rights is true. Yet it is also true that blacks believed in them so much and

so hard that we gave them life where there was none before."[65] For Williams, much like for Cox, rather than leading to moral relativism, centering accounts that have been ignored is key to advocacy, to highlighting both the interdependency of what is aboveboard and what is illegitimate, and the role of law in furthering this interdependency and its invisibility.

Like Williams, indigenous studies scholar Linda Tuhiwai Smith advocates writing "from that messy intersection, from the borders of the vast and expanding territory that is the margin, that exists 'outside' the security zone, outside the gated and fortified community."[66] For instance, Victoria Stone-Cadena and Soledad Álvarez Velasco study Indigenous Ecuadorians' understandings of *coyoterismo*, the practice of hiring smugglers, known as coyotes, to assist migrants in crossing borders without authorization.[67] In policy circles, coyotes have been depicted as ruthless profit-driven criminals who unscrupulously risk the lives of their clients. Yet as Stone-Cadena and Álvarez Velasco find, privileging Indigenous perspectives generates an alternative account. In Indigenous Ecuadoran communities, migration is a long-standing tradition, and labor opportunities and migrant remittances are critical to community well-being. As a result, migrants and their families rely on and appreciate the expertise and dedication of coyotes, who are themselves members of migrant communities. As one interviewee told the researchers, "Coyotes are part of us."[68] From "the margins," coyotes appear to be neither villains nor saviors but "an element within the continuum of migrants' decision-making, and in which migrants play clear and active roles."[69]

In our own research, privileging the accounts of adoptees and unauthorized migrants, who narratively theorize their own experiences, decenters the institutions that make them appear out of place. For example, in 2008 and again in 2010, Susan interviewed Araceli Muñoz, a temporary protected status recipient whose family immigrated to the United States when she was three years old, during the 1980–92 Salvadoran civil war. Araceli provided the following account of how she understood her connection to El Salvador:

> I mean, when people ask me, "Where's your family from?" or "Where are you from?" I say, "I'm from El Salvador" or "I was born there, but I grew up here." Like, I always feel like I have to make that distinction for some reason. I always say, "I was born there. I'm from there, technically, but I live here. I was raised here."
>
> And, I mean, we see things, like sometimes on the news that are—I'm not sure if you knew that, I think, a few years ago during the Rose Parade there was a band from El Salvador that came. And the entire time, we were thinking that maybe not a lot of people will show because we don't hear a lot of people saying, "Oh, I'm from El Salvador." We just kind of

think it's a few people. And then we go to the parade and there's like thousands and thousands of people and we're like, "Where do you guys all come from?" And, you know, it was kinda—I think, almost everywhere that whole week that they were here my, like, my family decided, "Let's go see where the kids are." They just kinda felt that connection, like, to see people from over there and I kinda went along and I saw them and everything, and I thought, you know, "Wow. It's great that people—younger people have a chance to come here and, you know, see." . . .

But they—there was a point where they [my family] were, like, saying—that they were playing some songs from over there that they've heard for, like, years and years and years. We've heard since we were kids also because they play it on the radio and stuff and they would just hear these songs that—they're, like, happy songs, but they just, like, started to cry and stuff. And me and my cousins—well, I'm the, like, I think—me and another one of my cousins are the only ones that were born here—were born there, I mean, and were raised here. All the rest of them were all born here, but then we saw our parents all crying and stuff and we just kinda looked at each other, like, "Oh, they're getting emotional." But we're just kinda standing there, like—we didn't really feel anything.

In this narrative, Araceli presents a fluid and multivalent analysis of origins and national affiliation. In contrast to the presumption that origins are singular, as is implied by the question "Where's your family from?" or "Where are you from?" Araceli describes having two origins: "El Salvador" and "here." Moreover, to Araceli, place of birth is a technical matter that may or may not reflect her own sense of belonging, a theme that she stressed in other parts of the conversation: "To me this is home. . . . I think it depends on where you grew up, where you spend most of your childhood, where . . . you learned what you know." When Araceli accompanied her relatives to the Rose Parade to hear a band from El Salvador perform, she was impressed to see "thousands and thousands" of other people from El Salvador turn out, but even though she knew the songs that the band performed, she and other family members of her generation, whether born in the United States or in El Salvador, lacked the emotional connection that her parents' generation had to the music. Belonging, in Araceli's theorization, has multiple dimensions: birth, familial relationships, residence, knowledge, socialization, and emotional connection. Overshadowing Araceli's account is law, which defined her at the time of our interview as only a temporary resident of the United States, the country that she described as "home." Araceli's nuanced account of belonging displays the artificiality of legal definitions that prioritize birthplace as a measure of nationality.

Shapeshifting Institutions of Kinship

Adults who were adopted as children also narrate their own theorizations of kinship experiences. In the case of transnational adoptees, such counternarratives aim at challenging the erasures of history that make transnational adoptions possible. In chapter 1, for example, we described a petition filed in 2018 by the AEF in Stockholm with the Swedish parliament, requesting a paradigm shift in that nation's approach to adoption. The AEF asked Sweden to recognize that adoptees' lives begin with birth, a recognition that would effectively nullify the key premise of adoption practice, namely that the adopted child is an as-if-begotten child, and that the only parent is the adoptive parent. This petition emerged from the experiences of Swedish adoptees from Ethiopia, such as Sara Nordin, who described what it meant to her, as the Swedish daughter of white parents, to *become* Black. In an essay that was published in *Svart/Vitt*, a Swedish journal of race relations, Nordin wrote:

> BLACK!
> The meaning of this word has grown with each passing year, until I have finally understood that I am black. It is something big, personal, and hard. It is a fact for me.
> The people who only see my color don't see all of me. The people who suggest they can see beyond my color don't see all of me. When I try to gather together all the bits of myself, I easily lose myself. In colors and stories. In theories and dreams. When I go by the mirror I see something exotic that I barely recognize from TV, newspapers, and books. Sometimes it makes me happy, sometimes sad, and sometimes amazed. But most often the reflection in the mirror evokes questions that have no easy answers.
> I have tried to absorb the "black' but then I have difficulty holding onto the Swedish. I have tried to absorb the "Swedish" but then I haven't understood what I see in the mirror.[70]

Sara's struggle to come to terms with what it meant to be both Black and Swedish was brought to a head when she visited the Kebebe Tsehay orphanage in Addis Ababa in her mid-twenties and found her name in the orphanage registry, as discussed in chapter 1. During a conversation in her Stockholm apartment in 2015, she explained to Barbara, "Just that I found my name there turned my world upside down." She added, "I have now been back six or seven times, and each trip has given me a new key to myself and my relationship to that country."

The experiences of Ethiopian adoptees were particularly fraught in the 1980s and 1990s, a time when Sweden was establishing its own identity as a global model for social justice and racial equality, with the transracially adopted child as "some kind of token," in the words of Amanda Fredricksson, a friend of Sara's who was also adopted from Ethiopia. As Amanda characterized Sweden's transracial adoption policy in an interview with Barbara in 2002, "For heaven's sake! We can at least show people that one can have a child that doesn't look like oneself! And so one should be some kind of means of social change." While adoptees of African descent were perceived (by themselves and others) as the most visible indicators of such openness to racialized difference in Sweden, the petition filed by the AEF with the Swedish parliament in 2018 spoke more broadly to a collective effort on the part of Swedish transracial adoptees to give voice to the failure of a model of social change in which those who are adopted serve as a visible token of difference in adoptive families but must become the same (as them) for the adoption to succeed.[71]

Sara articulated an alternative vision in a 1999 interview with Barbara, in which she spoke about the radical shapeshifting that was needed on the part of adoption organizations, the Swedish National Board for Intercountry Adoptions (NIA), and specifically adoptive parents if there was to be meaningful change in the increasingly racialized dynamics that were consuming Swedish society at the turn of the twenty-first century. This shift involved the very shape of the Swedish adoptive family and the assumptions that defined its completeness. As Sara argued, "I feel that it is important, when one adopts, that one realizes, 'I didn't give birth to this child, but the child had a history already and must have its own history the whole time, without my attempting to transform this into our history. It's the child's and that is fine; it is something positive, not something tragic.'"

This counternarrative to the widespread belief in Sweden as color-blind, the African child as the adoptive parents' "dream child," and, most centrally, the assumption that the birth parent and birth nation are irrelevant to the adoptive family and the best interest of the child, was put on display publicly for the first time in a collective performance of some 120 adult adoptees at a meeting of the board of directors of Sweden's principal adoption organization, Adoption Centre (AC), in 1997.[72] The adoptees, who had grown up in Sweden, Denmark, and Norway in the 1970s, 1980s, and 1990s, were invited to attend a series of workshops on the theme of "roots and returns" (resor och rötter), to be held in parallel with AC's annual meeting of its board of directors, which was composed primarily of adoptive parents. The unarticulated but powerful subtext of the workshops was the racism confronting transnational adoptees not only in Sweden but elsewhere in Scandinavia, a topic increasingly addressed in the essays, memoirs, and academic writings of adult adoptees.[73]

The watershed moment at the workshop series (known as Forum '97) was the dramatic entry of workshop participants into the AC board meeting, each wearing a white shirt with a large Swedish flag printed on the front. After they had all filed onto a stage in the auditorium where the parents were gathered, they turned in unison to display the words that each had hand-printed on the back of their Swedish-themed shirts: "MADE IN [KOREA, ETHIOPIA, COLOMBIA, CHILE, NEPAL]" and so forth, for each birth country in which the adult who had been adopted was "made." The moment of turning was greeted with laughter and applause by the parents. It captured the ambiguities of a discourse of identity represented by the adoptees—an identity that was located neither inside nor completely outside the Swedish families that they, in turn, had made but in a rapidly developing transformation at the very core of what it meant to be Swedish in the late twentieth century.[74] This reconfiguration of the essence of the Swedish as shaped in a world made by adoption was to expand in the next two decades as growing numbers of adopted adults returned to the countries where they were born, in search of answers to questions about why they were adopted and who they were before the legal procedure that transformed them into Swedish people. It was this expanded territory that the AEF sought to buttress with legal scaffolding in its petitions to the Swedish parliament in 2018.

Like Araceli's nuanced analysis of the multidimensionality of origins and the challenge this analysis presents to official definitions that prioritize only birthplace as home in the United States, transnationally adopted adults like Sara Nordin, Amanda Fredricksson, and other participants at the Forum '97 workshops sought to make visible the multidimensionality of home for adopted people, while expanding the meaning of family in Sweden to include the histories of adopted children. The Forum '97 performance provided a moment of collective empowerment that came from both articulating and transgressing the limited social scripts that were provided for transnationally adopted children and adults in the second half of the twentieth century, both in Sweden and elsewhere. These scripts focused on what was defined by adoption professionals as the child's best interest, but in practice these officials were attentive more to what were presumed to be the needs of the adopting parents and adoptive nations for exclusive rights to adopted children. This assumption about children's best interests, and the policies that accompanied it, also led to the pathologizing of adoptees who failed to adapt to such scripts, rather than to an examination of how adoption policies, and specifically the legal fictions of orphan status and as-if-genealogical belonging, might affect the well-being of those who were adopted.[75] In this regard, the efforts of Nordin and other members of the AEF represent a key intervention in Swedish adoption policy by privileging the history of each child rather than canceling that history in favor of making the adoptive family complete in itself.

Revisioning Fields

As ethnographers seeking to document conflicting accounts of what counts as an origin or as home for the unauthorized or the adopted, we found ourselves engaged in forms of shapeshifting that at times evoked those of our interlocutors. In Barbara's case, this shapeshifting was a dimension of her complex positioning in a potential space in which her history as an adoptive mother in an open domestic adoption in the United States connected her in different (and sometimes conflicting) ways to the adoptive parents who founded AC in Sweden, on the one hand, and to the transnationally adopted adults who were seeking their roots in the countries where they were born, on the other. For adoptees, it was the open dimension of Barbara's identity as an adoptive mother that became the ground for their relationship to her as interlocutors, a relationship in which she was entrusted with their life stories as a way of documenting the realities they lived in and the fears they harbored as adoptees. Their willingness to recount these stories for the purposes of her research were contingent (as least in part) on her willingness to use these stories as a means of shifting the shape of transnational adoption policy toward an acknowledgment of the multidimensionality of belongings for those who are adopted, both in Sweden and as a global practice. In this sense, her positioning as a researcher/adoptive mother who was embedded at AC and shadowed its representatives in their travels to Asia and Latin America in the pursuit of adoptable children for Swedish families complicated and potentially compromised her engagement with the projects of more activist adoptees, such as those in the AEF and in the Forum '97 workshops (although this concern was never made explicit to Barbara). Whose team was she on? And how might information she acquired in one adoption context be deployed in another?

At AC, Barbara's focus on the negotiation of motherhood in open adoptions in her earlier research and particularly her acknowledgment of her son's birth mother as (also) his mother were received with skepticism on the grounds that it could only lead to confusion for the adopted child. Nonetheless, senior staff at the organization made use of her expertise in the expanding field of open adoptions in the United States in order to mediate their increasingly strained relationship to activist adult adoptees who sought to pursue ongoing relationships with their first families. Such relationships were seen as compromising the "completeness" of the adoptees' transformation into Swedish persons whose adoptive parents were, in the eyes of AC staff and by law, their only "real" parents. For adoptees, by contrast, and especially for Barbara's interlocutors in the AEF, her attempts to live with the paradoxes of a form of motherhood that was simultaneously real and not real, licit and illicit, and to straddle the uneasy boundary that connected relationships in her field of research to relationships that were not research, including her lived relationship of adoptive kinship, positioned her within the context of a process of shapeshifting in which they themselves were constantly engaged. In this sense, in spite of the vast differences that separated their lives from hers (and most notably the key place of race in the lives of Ethiopian and other transracial adoptees), she found a sense of familiarity in the pattern that emerged in their struggles with conventional understandings of what constituted family and the meanings of home.

Susan, too, engaged in a kind of shapeshifting throughout her ethnographic research. She was originally pulled into research regarding immigration policy through the 1980s sanctuary movement, a grassroots network of congregations that declared themselves sanctuaries for Salvadoran and Guatemalan refugees. At the time, Susan was a graduate student immersed in critiques of anthropology's colonial roots, so she eschewed the model of research in which ethnographers live within another community in order to write about its way of life. Instead, she positioned herself as a solidarity worker writing about other solidarity workers, a community to which she belonged. Much of her ethnographic research consisted of volunteering with the movement, and in that sense, it was indistinguishable from the activities of other movement members. In fact, she remembers vividly (and somewhat guiltily) a comment made by one movement member: "What I admire about you is that you go to *all* of the events!" Over the years, she maintained this engaged approach to research, collaborating with Central American community organizations; assisting in preparing applications for asylum, DACA, and other forms of relief; and supporting organizations' events, while also conducting interviews, following networks, shadowing service providers, participating in events, and observing hearings. Throughout, she often wondered about the compatibility of these roles. Was she fraudulently claiming to be an ethnographer while in fact primarily serving as a volunteer who was clearly committed to advocating with and for immigrants and asylum seekers? Or was her involvement in movement and NGO activities fraudulent, a means of gaining access and securing information? Or both and neither at the same time?

Through her engagement with Central American organizations and immigration policy, Susan constructed fields that coincided only loosely with bounded groups of people. These fields—networks of activists, asylum seekers and their attorneys, government officials in the United States and El Salvador, writers and artists, other academics, and transnational circuits of migration and activism—existed before and continued after her ethnographic endeavors but were also assemblages that she interacted with for particular projects. Even though she adopted engaged approaches, she felt very much like an outsider: a highly privileged person who had not had to migrate or seek asylum, at least not yet, and who had not experienced the kind of over-policing that can make communities of color subject to criminalization and illegalization. What, she wondered, gave her the right or even the ability to say anything meaningful about the experiences of those who live in the United States as undocumented immigrants, or the attorneys and activists who represent them?

While this sort of angst is not unusual among ethnographers, we revisit it here in order to consider the ways that such questions shapeshift both the institution of ethnography and practices of home making in the ways that we have explicated in this chapter. Entanglement—with interlocutors, colleagues, and topics—is a fraught experience, positioning ethnographers and interlocutors within and outside fields at the same time. Staying with this fraught experience instead of attempting to erase it, resolve it, or turn it into something else generates the sort of fieldsight that comes from "seeing simultaneously yet differently," to again quote Patricia Williams. Ethnographers both are and are not fraudulent; we do and do not have the ability to present ethnographic truths that we encounter and construct through fieldwork. Entanglement disrupts linear notions of time and muddies clear demarcations of space, as one moment seeps into another and futures are revisited in the past. In fact, fieldsight in some ways depends on that which lies outside the domain of inquiry as well as that which is within the ethnographer. Fieldwork establishes a productive, paradoxical, and fluid relationship between existent and nonexistent realities. The activities and relationships forged during fieldwork have other meanings as well: an interlocutor can also be a friend, a relative, or a coworker. Just as, in Bateson's words, "play is a phenomenon in which the actions of 'play' are related to, or denote, other actions of 'not play,'" so too do the actions of fieldwork denote other actions of not fieldwork, and vice versa.[76] For example, during fieldwork, speech acts may denote a conversation, but because ethnographers may view comments as data to be recorded in fieldnotes, these speech acts do not mean what a conversation normally means. Because the relationship between fieldwork and non-fieldwork is ambiguous and shifting, ethnographers have to wrestle with certain dilemmas: Is this fieldwork? What are the boundaries of my research?

The fluid position that makes it possible to re-vision fieldwork also privileges the theoretical insights of interlocutors. Just as Cox's ethnography presented Janice's and other shelter residents' critiques of pathologizing discourses, and just as Barbara's work highlighted critiques by transnational adoptees of as-if-genealogical belonging in favor of a more inclusive understanding of what makes a family complete, so too do the theoretical insights of immigrants and advocates challenge the legal system that treats border control as a matter of national sovereignty. For Katarina, instead of creating orderly categorizations, US immigration laws produce a void in which "there is nothing here, there is nothing there." Likewise, Diana highlighted the invisibility of women who work in homes—who could be considered essential workers—and who lack documentation of their presence in the United States. Araceli Muñoz also questioned the accuracy of legal definitions, which might highlight only one dimension of belonging, such as birthplace, to the exclusion of social ties, emotional connection, and length of residence. Katarina, Diana, and Araceli theorize law as a system that produces disorder, injustice, and misrecognition. In their accounts, much like the counternarrative presented by Patricia Williams, positionings can be fluid, origins can be multiple, and home can transcend boundaries.

"The Truth in the Documentary"

> All science is an attempt to cover with explanatory devices—and thereby to obscure—the vast darkness of the subject. It is a game in which the scientist uses his explanatory principles according to certain rules to see if these principles can be stretched to cover the vast darkness. But the rules of the stretching are rigorous, and the purpose of the whole operation is really to discover what parts of the darkness still remain, uncovered by explanation.
>
> Gregory Bateson, *Naven*

A final example of double vision and the invisible realities it brings to light involves what Gianfranco Rosi describes as "the truth in the documentary" and what we are suggesting can be captured with the concept of fieldsight in ethnographic research.[77] Rosi suggests that the process of creating truth is contingent on moments of revelation, when "I follow my instinct to put the camera there at the right moment and to create trust." He goes on: "If there's no trust, there's nothing. In fact, people ask me: 'How do you disappear in your films?' But I don't disappear, I'm constantly there. I'm the one who interacts with them. It takes two people to create that. And at that moment, I change, and they change, and the camera is changing everything and transforming reality into something else. There's a constant transformation of reality into something else in my films. . . . When the camera is there, things are going to change."[78]

This process of transforming reality into something else is especially evident in Rosi's relationship with twelve-year-old Samuele Pucillo, who spends his free time whittling slingshots so that he can kill songbirds and painting fields of cactuses with "the face of the enemy" so that he can destroy them with firecrackers. Juxtaposing shots of the Italian coastguard processing the dead and injured bodies of North African asylum seekers with Samuele's games of destruction among the flora and fauna of Lampedusa leads Rosi to a representation of Samuele as the island's subconscious and to a powerful depiction of the entanglement of islanders and migrants, even as they seemingly inhabit disconnected worlds. At the same time, Rosi's own distance from the world of the migrants, and his implicit complicity in the system that processes them, is revealed as a truth of the film, as suggested by the journalist and film critic Yonka Talu, who observed to Rosi during a 2016 interview: "For me, the most devastating images of the film are those of migrants looking into your lens, when they realize they're being filmed."[79] Noting that this reminded her of images of Holocaust survivors staring into the camera in Antoine de Baecque's book *Camera Historica*, Talu suggests that "the looks in your film made me feel the same way, as though I was staring at the face of death, as though cinema had to change."[80] In response, Rosi explained to Talu: "For me, it was a big challenge to decide to film this. I had to show that in the back of these numbers, they're human beings, that there's inspiration, fear, and hope in their eyes. When they are in front of the camera, or when they are getting searched and they look at me, in this moment, I am somehow part of the system. My camera embodies the [rescue/detention] system there."[81]

This exchange highlights a key tension in *Fire at Sea*, in which the dynamics of presence and absence (of the filmmaker or ethnographer) are in complex relationship to the dynamics of presence and absence of the subjects. Talu's reference to the "devastating images . . . of migrants looking into your lens, when they realize they're being filmed," and Rosi's acknowledgment that in that moment, "I am somehow part of the system," reveal the extent to which the potential space in which Rosi's camerawork unfolds is defined by the very divisions he is seeking to overcome. It also highlights the ways in which "the system" (of relationships, as defined by colonialism and its aftermath) affects the intimacy of his coverage of Samuele and the island doctor, for example, in contrast to "the ritual of death, the song of death," and "the face of death" that Rosi, the doctor, and the coast guard see when the migrants are "in front of the camera" and that comes into play in Samuele's games as he "builds the face of the enemy" so that he can destroy that as-if enemy with his slingshot.[82]

Rosi's aim in *Fire at Sea* is to bridge the divide between the world of the migrants and the world of the islanders by using his camera as a tool for revealing "the truth that belongs so intimately to each of them,"[83] while avoiding objectifying representations. As a reflection of the challenges he encountered in doing so, the truth of the migrants makes itself known only obliquely in the film: in their silent but intense gaze as they look into Rosi's camera, in the chant of suffering and death of Nigerian refugees in the holding center, and, most harrowingly, in a mass rescue operation by the Italian coast guard toward the end of the film. The wonder of appearance of this truth is signaled in the recurrence of technologies that illuminate the "vast darkness" that seems to surround it.[84] Rather than presenting to viewers a single truth for their contemplation, Rosi creates a "state of interpretation" in which viewers are invited to participate, suggesting that the complex truths that lie at the heart of the migrant crisis may lie concealed as well in the hearts of viewers of this film, and the film provides revelatory moments in which these truths may be brought to light.[85]

SCHRÖDINGER'S CAT

The "Missing Middle," Discredited Histories,
and Measurement Problems

> The way we always have to think about how other people see us and
> compare it to how we see ourselves. . . . They [TV, papers] miss the
> middle because they are always focused on the outside and making
> assumptions about who we are. There's a lot in the middle, but
> who's trying to see that?
>
> Aimee Marie Cox, *Shapeshifters: Black Girls and the Choreography of
> Citizenship*, quoting Janice, a resident of Fresh Start Homeless Shelter
> in Detroit, Michigan

In this chapter, we take up "the middle" in order to consider the multiple locations
and temporalities of both ethnography and law.[1] In so doing, we seek an alternative to the seemingly dichotomous possibilities that ethnography and law either
discover or invent/construct social reality. The notion of discovery of course characterizes positivist notions of empiricism, whereas the notion of invention, that
ethnographies are in some sense fictions or constructions that can be read alongside other cultural products, grew out of critiques of positivism developed during
the 1980s.[2] Instead of revisiting such debates to take one side or the other, we
suggest that law and ethnography *both* discover *and* invent in that legal and ethnographic accounts retroactively instantiate realities that potentially existed all
along.[3] Such realities open up the middle that is "missed" when the media, law, or
ethnography focus on what Janice describes as "the outside and making assumptions about who we are."

By narrating versions of reality that are there all along but that, without official
recognition, remain potentialities, ethnographers bring alternative and conventional realities into play with each other while underscoring the "as-ifness" of conventional worlds and their contingency on invisible ones. Notably, such narrations,
whether performed by ethnographers or legal actors, enable social or legal reality
to resolve itself into a single outcome. Indeed, we suggest here that the fictions that
make fieldwork possible—the moments of substitution, for instance, in which
fieldnotes come to stand in for events, and quotations come to stand in for

fieldnotes—may enhance rather than undermine ethnography's capacity to convey complex social truths. Such moments are condensations, "meetings between two separate moments that come together to form a new intensity," or translations that make possible ethnography's ability to approximate the real, as we discussed in chapter 1.[4] Similarly, legal judgments are based on evidence even as they select among potential interpretations of legal facts. Of course, there are points at which the analogy between law and ethnography breaks down, when, for example, one contrasts the power of a legal verdict with the power of an ethnographic account. The former can result in incarceration, liberation, death, or the transfer of property, whereas the latter does not usually have such dire consequences—though there have been instances of collaboration between anthropologists and military campaigns.[5] Our analogy between ethnography, law, and, to a lesser degree, quantum physics (discussed in the next section) indicate that "each of the possibilities— each of the possible histories—contributes to what we now observe."[6] As they instantiate potential realities, ethnographers become privy to those that were not realized and that in retrospect can be seen as discredited histories or unreal events. As a consequence of this binocular vision, ethnography itself, and the fields that materialize in its wake, move.

The Cat in the Box

An example of the fraught relationship between an authorized or officially measured reality and the indeterminacy of the potential realities out of which the official real takes shape is the infamous thought experiment proposed by physicist Erwin Schrödinger and known as Schrödinger's paradox.[7] In an attempt to demonstrate the absurdity of the argument that physical reality, until measured, is indeterminate, Schrödinger invited his readers to imagine that there is a box containing a photon source, a slanted translucent mirror, a gun, and a cat. After the box is shut, a single photon is released in the direction of the mirror. The probability that the photon will pass through the mirror is precisely 50 percent. If the photon does not pass through the mirror, it will be reflected toward the bottom of the box. On the other hand, if the photon does pass through the mirror, it will cause the gun to release a pellet of poisonous gas, killing the cat. Without opening the box, it is impossible to know whether the cat is alive or dead. Similarly, according to quantum physics, the location of an electron (or photon) is best represented by a probability that takes the form of a wave. If the location or path of the electron is actually measured in a laboratory, then this wave function collapses into certainty. If it is *not* measured, however, experiments suggest that the electron occupies multiple potential locations *at the same time*: "It is not that the electron (or any particle for that matter) really was located at only one of these possible positions, but we simply don't know which. Rather, there is a sense in which the electron was at all of the locations, because each of the possibilities—each of the possible histories—contributes to what we now observe."[8] Thus, in the case of the thought experiment, until the box is opened, the photon may have gone multiple ways, leaving the cat in a state of alive-deadness that, upon being observed, resolves itself into a single photon path and into life or death. It was this prior indeterminacy (the alive-dead cat, the multiple simultaneous paths of a single photon—a state now known in quantum physics as "entanglement") that Schrödinger found absurd.[9]

This quantum physics problem of the relationship between a measured outcome and the much more contingent (and varied) history that resulted in that outcome also characterizes both law and ethnography. For example, when a US immigration judge awards political asylum to an applicant, events that the asylum seeker experienced in the past officially resolve themselves into persecution. Note that this resolution of a more ambiguous reality is the *opposite* of how law is supposed to work. The determination that an individual deserves political asylum is supposed to simply affirm that the individual *was already* persecuted (or had a well-founded fear of persecution). Prior to the judge's ruling, however, the legal definition of these events was in contention, and had the judge ruled otherwise, the events in question would not have been officially deemed persecution (at least until appealed). Similarly, when a probate judge grants an adoption decree to parents in the United States, events that a birth mother experienced in the past as giving birth retroactively turn out legally to be nonevents. Thus, when Jan Waldron, a woman who placed her infant daughter for adoption in 1969, contacted the town hall twenty-three years later in the city where she had given birth, she was told that there was no record of the birth. "At the legal moment of adoption, explained the clerk of the court, the birth certificate was 'filled out as if her adoptive parents were her parents, y'know, the real parents, the natural ones.'"[10] At the hospital where her daughter was born, there were records of the infant's birth, but no cross-reference with the mother's file. Her daughter Rebecca "had been born, yes, but there was no evidence that a mother, I, had brought her into existence."[11] Giving birth turns out to be a contingent process that, until legally measured, may or may not have officially occurred (or may have occurred *and* not occurred).[12]

Ethnographies, too, select a particular path among processes that, while unfolding, are somewhat fortuitous potentialities. Thus, while ethnographers collect data in order to answer research questions that motivate a particular study, ethnographers must simultaneously remain open to possibilities that had not occurred to them before they entered the field and that, in fact, may not be considered as having occurred prior to the ethnography being written. Such openness is a key feature of fieldsight, as we discussed in chapter 2. The need to remain open to the possibility that the field may be reconfigured as the results of fieldwork take shape poses a conundrum not unlike that confronted by the physicist attempting to reconcile probability and outcome, or the legal analyst attempting to align judgment and history. Ethnographers must reconcile the veracity of ethnographic accounts with ethnographers' own (re)constructions of the field during fieldwork. As ethnographer Marilyn Strathern asks, "How does one argue back from an unforeseen event, an unpredictable outcome, to the circumstances of its development?"[13]

Thought Experiments

At approximately the same time that physicist Erwin Schrödinger developed the Schrödinger's cat thought experiment, anthropologist Gregory Bateson was pursuing a sort of thought experiment of his own as he carried out fieldwork among the Iatmul of Papua New Guinea. Bateson was fascinated with double vision, an interest he attributes to habits of mind he acquired implicitly from his father, a geneticist, who "had always a hankering after the problems of pattern and symmetry."[14] For Bateson, who was trained as a biologist but had to figure out how to be an anthropologist when he went to New Guinea, this hankering and the "mystical belief in the pervading unity of the phenomena of the world" were both necessary for science.[15] He explained, "When I was analyzing the patterns of partridges' feathers, I might really get an answer or a bit of an answer to the whole puzzling business of pattern and regularity in nature."[16] His commitment to science led Bateson to develop "this double habit of mind—it led me into wild 'hunches,' and, at the same time, compelled more formal thinking about those hunches. It encouraged looseness of thought and then immediately insisted that looseness be measured up against a rigid concreteness."[17]

As Bateson collected ethnographic data, such as fieldnotes, photographs, and verbatim summaries of informants' accounts, he was also continually pulled by that which was not (or not yet) data, spinning elaborate theories of "schismogenesis"—"*a process of differentiation in the norms of individual behaviour resulting from cumulative interaction between individuals*"—and cultural change out of material he described as insufficient.[18] *Naven*, Bateson's ethnography of the Iatmul, is organized around something of a puzzle: Why do the Iatmul have a ceremony that features transvesticism, in which men dress in women's ragged clothes and women dress in men's finery? Furthermore, why is this ceremony filled with buffoonery and eroticism? To answer these questions, Bateson attempted to divide Iatmul culture into various components—"ethos, eidos, sociology, economics, cultural structure, social structure"—only to discover, after he completed his book, that any element of Iatmul culture could be placed in any of these categories.[19] Figure and ground continually shift within *Naven*, as Bateson describes events that he recorded yet is equally drawn to what he had backgrounded while in the field: the implicit, or what was sensed or felt rather than directly observed or known.

An example of the value of implicit or emotional knowledge is provided by Bateson's explanation of how "one detail of the Palimbai *naven*"—the observation that transvestite *waus* (mother's brother and related male figures) were "figures of fun"—led him to a realization: "My whole mental picture of *naven* had been wrong, and wrong because, though I had been told what was done, I had no idea of the emotional aspects of the behavior."[20] As a result of this discovery of emotional content, he "came to believe that ethos was the *thing* that mattered."[21] Much later, after his return to England, he similarly drew on knowledge from outside his fieldwork in order to deepen his understanding. While looking at photographs from his fieldwork, he noticed that for public ceremonies, Iatmul women wear ornaments typically worn only by men, a discovery that in turn suggested to him the potential parallel of the Iatmul phenomenon with "the fashionable [British] horsewoman," something he had not studied.[22] The horsewoman provided a "hint of the sort of situation . . . in which partial transvesticism occurs, namely in the case of women who take part in spectacular ceremonies."[23] Bateson suggests that it was from what he later came to describe as "abduction," or the "lateral extension of abstract components of description," that his theory of Iatmul transvesticism emerged.[24] That theory, however was eventually itself backgrounded, as the paper in which he presented it "grew by the addition first of one method of approach and then of another, until it has become the present book, and now its purpose is no longer to put forward a theory of Iatmul transvesticism, but to suggest methods of thinking about anthropological problems."[25]

Gregory Bateson describes such movement between frames of perception, and the fieldsight that accompanies them, as "*a zig-zag ladder of dialectic between form and process*," and associates it with the insights provided by hunches, implicit knowledge, and the unobservable "feel" of a culture when these are coupled with observations and recorded accounts.[26] Likewise, the body of Bateson's work following his research in Papua New Guinea suggests that such a dialectic, and its transgression of the limits of rote empiricism, is incredibly generative. Thus, even as ethnographers attempt to bound their studies by delimiting a particular field of inquiry, they may also analyze that which is outside that field (an unuttered statement or an event that went unobserved or was seemingly part of an unrelated field, such as the insight provided by the example of the British horsewoman).

Fieldsight's dependence on that which lies outside the domain of inquiry—seeing beyond the obvious, a leap of faith—suggests that fieldwork "relies on the element of play, in both of its two senses, that of *looseness*, as in the play of a key in a lock . . . and in the sense of a *game*, one in which we have to be ready to perceive unexpected opportunities in what before was rigidified."[27] Bateson saw play as a metamessage, "the name of a *frame* for action" rather than "the name of an act or action."[28] As a frame for action, play has "a special and peculiar relationship to reality."[29] That is, the message "this is play" sets the frame for "integrations of behavior which a) do not define the actions which are their content; and b) do not obey the ordinary enforcement rules."[30] Play incorporates elements of ritual (e.g., rules) even as "it retains some elements of the creative and unexpected," as suggested, for example, in Rosi's depiction of Samuele's games involving songbirds and cactuses in *Fire at Sea*, as discussed in chapter 2.[31]

Like play, fieldwork establishes a productive, paradoxical, and fluid relationship between existent and nonexistent realities. Bateson notes that play has two peculiarities: "(a) that the messages or signals exchanged in play are in a certain sense untrue or not meant; and (b) that that which is denoted by these signals is nonexistent."[32] These peculiarities characterize fieldwork as well. An ethnographer's presence at an event signals participation, but the ethnographer may also be an observer. Hence, the message signaled by participation may not be meant and the effects that participation would have created may not be realized. The frame "this is fieldwork" also differentiates figure from ground: "Figure and ground, as these terms are used by gestalt psychologists, are not symmetrically related as are the set and nonset of set theory. Perception of the ground must be positively inhibited and perception of the figure (in this case the picture) must be positively enhanced."[33] The frame of "field" directs ethnographers' attention to the figure—the set of activities and so on that are "data"—and away from the "ground"—that which is outside the field. Yet, the relationship between "play" and "not play," or "field" and "non-fieldwork" is ambiguous and shifting. For instance, an ethnographer may attend a political protest as an observer but the ethnographer's self-proclaimed observer status will not prevent the ethnographer from being arrested and having a subsequent court case.

As a research method, ethnography relies on the as if—in some cases, ethnographers act as if they were a member of a given culture, or in other cases act as if they were *not* a member. As they act as if, ethnographers put their faculties at the disposal of the field of inquiry that they have created. Thus, Bateson's participation in Iatmul social life *did* define him as a quasi-member of an Iatmul clan: "Certain male natives who regarded me as their classificatory 'sister's child' on the basis of a matrilineal name which had been given to me, used occasionally to refer to themselves as my 'mothers' when stressing their kinship connection with me. One of them would even say to me: 'You are the child that we bore.' ('We' here refers to the maternal clan.) At other times informants would refer to the clan, whose matrilineal name I bore, with such a phrase as 'They are your mother.'"[34] This passage appears in *Naven* as data, as part of an explanation of the Iatmul's kinship system, thus demonstrating how the nonexistent reality (Bateson's relationship to members of a matrilineal kin group) created by the frame "this is fieldwork" is also ethnographically productive (it teaches him about kinship). The activities that enable fieldsight only have meaning in the configuration of a field, in the sense of both a discipline and a site.

Multidimensionality of the kinds discussed here creates an implied yet fictitious interchangeability between ethnographers and readers. A footnote in *Naven* states, "Among the Iatmul one often hears . . ."[35] But of course, at the time of his research, "one" (Bateson's readership) was most likely *not* among the Iatmul. Interchangeability contributes to dynamic temporality, which disorders linear accounts of time.[36] As Elspeth Probyn argues, the "surface" is not merely "superficial" but also undergirded by a "deep historicity."[37] Understanding this historicity—how knowledge was created, the nature of underlying structures—requires going below the surface, as "organisms [tend] toward sinking into the unconscious those generalities of relationship which remain permanently true and toward keeping within the conscious the pragmatics of particular instances."[38] In so doing, ethnographers may experience the "vast darkness" of the subjects that they attempt to explicate.[39]

Collections and Juxtapositions

One way of entering this "vast darkness" and revealing more general but invisible patterns that lie beneath the surface is the practice of "double or multiple description of some object or event or sequence."[40] *Naven* emerged from just such a practice, in which the particularities of the collection that took shape as data for that project included (retroactively) a crucial insight supplied by Bateson's discovery of similarities between the attire of a British horsewoman and a Palimbai *wau*. In our own collaboration, we have included an unpredictable collection of actors, events, and observations as we move back and forth between material on immigration, transnational adoption, and political disappearances. This mode of collaboration differs from comparison, in which similarities and differences between phenomena, cases, or situations are identified in order to decipher the broader processes that are producing these similarities and differences and, in some instances, to predict or shape future outcomes.[41]

In contrast to deliberate comparison, our collaboration emerged somewhat fortuitously when, along with our colleague Bill Maurer—professor of anthropology at the University of California, Irvine—we discovered that we could translate among our respective analyses of transnational adoption, unauthorized migration, and offshore finance. When we read the papers that we each had prepared for a session at the 1998 Law and Society Association meeting in Aspen, Colorado, we found that we could substitute different terms for sentences in one another's drafts and that the sentences would still make sense:

> Offshore transactions originate, precisely, "offshore," somewhere else, a space imagined to lie outside of powerful sovereign states.
>
> Transnational adoption originates, precisely, in a natural "real," somewhere else, a space imagined to lie outside of law.
>
> Unauthorized migration occurs, precisely, "underground," somewhere else, a space imagined to lie outside of powerful sovereign territories.

This realization led us to write a joint article in which we each wrote not only our own but also each other's data.[42] We were able to do so partly because we were very familiar with one another's work but also because we came to know the phenomena that we had not studied through those with which we were already familiar. In other words, we proceeded less through comparison than through analogy and translation.

Similarly, the two of us subsequently wrote an article analyzing roots trips, which transnational adoptees make to their birth countries, and deportations in which Salvadoran immigrants are forcibly returned to their country of citizenship.[43] It seemed obvious to us that juxtaposing these two phenomena would reveal complexities of such journeys "back" and ways that law assigns and erases origins. Some reviewers and colleagues observed, however, that these phenomena were not comparable (a criticism that we had also received regarding the joint paper that we wrote with Bill Maurer). We concluded, then, that roots trips and deportations were neither intrinsically analogous nor intrinsically incomparable.[44] Rather, they are rendered analogous by the relationships that juxtaposition brings into being. These relationships are fictions, akin to legal fictions, not in the sense of something that is false or invented but in the sense that they are necessary for reality to assume its observable form. The relationships brought into being through juxtaposition are therefore not unlike the multiple simultaneous paths of a photon or unrealized versions of social reality that are not recorded in fieldnotes or quoted in a published work but that nonetheless make ethnography possible. In a similar way, as we discuss in the next section, people who are deported or adopted also engage in juxtaposition, as they encounter selves and lives that were rendered invisible through the legal decrees that made them who they are today.

Rather than advocating particular approaches to gathering data, our purpose here is to theorize the relationship between ethnographic accounts and the necessarily somewhat contingent process of data collection that is made possible by fieldsight. Although most noticeable in extreme situations, this dimension of fieldwork is central to the ethnographic project, in which the ethnographer is positioned at the "missing middle" between worlds, where familiar stereotypes break down in the context of powerful but "uncategorizable" experiences.[45] Fieldsight, as we argued in chapter 2, is an effect of putting disparate or incompatible experiences into relationship with one another in such a way as to create a potential space in which new understandings can materialize.

Oscillation

Bringing together roots trips and deportations involved a double translation and collection: the initial period of data collection on roots trips and on deportations, and a second process in which roots trips were juxtaposed to deportations and became a new collection of sorts. In the second period, we were brought up against a problem of comparison: as we thought roots trips through the frame of a deportation and vice versa, what we had imagined to be the ground of each (an origin point in a birth country or in an adopted country) shifted because of its newly apparent connection to the other. Deportation became the half-hidden counterpart of adoption and the roots trips that followed; adoption became the half-hidden counterpart to deportation, emphasizing deportation's specific "path of flight."[46] This revelation—that a deportation is a kind of shadow other to a roots trip (and vice versa)—suggested both their inseparability and why they cannot be compared. Adoption and deportation proved to be unstable, oscillating objects of study. Like the process of gathering data in a field, where one's interlocutors might be pulling in unexpected directions, our juxtapositional project pulled us to discoveries of information in our material that we would have overlooked had we not immersed ourselves in each other's field of data and been forced to struggle with the forms that adoption and immigration took (in relation to each other) in this engagement.

Examining each of these processes vis-à-vis the other was revelatory not only for our interpretation of roots trips and deportations but also for our understanding of the implications of each in securing the foundational figures of liberal law: the "natural" child, the "native-born" citizen. If "natural" children and citizens can be alienated through adoption or emigration, then both kinship and citizenship are potentially ephemeral and in need of the anchoring provided by adoptions and emigrations. Indeed, adoptions and emigrations realize these "natural" figures retroactively, much as, upon measurement, a photon's travels resolve themselves into a singular path, and Schrödinger's cat is revealed to be dead or alive when the box is opened. Note, however, that our analysis reverses conventional understandings, in which it is the "natural" child and the "native-born" citizen that anchor the as-if worlds of adopted children and naturalized citizens. As Benjamin notes, "Translation, ironically, transplants the original into a more definitive linguistic real."[47]

An example of such oscillation, and of the complex ways that adoption and deportation shadow each other, is provided by the following excerpt from an interview with Greg, a man who was adopted to the United States from El Salvador as a child and was subsequently deported to El Salvador because of a criminal conviction. His deportation was an effect of the law's failure to naturalize him as a US citizen. But because his adoption naturalized him as the child of US parents (but not as a citizen of the United States), Greg's "return" to El Salvador placed him in a space where he was not viable. Although technically a Salvadoran citizen, Greg was alienated from El Salvador and, in effect, had no country.[48]

The excerpt that follows from Susan's interviews with Greg suggests the implications of deportation and adoption for making and unmaking not only juridical but "natural" personhood as well. The interview took place in El Salvador, following Greg's deportation:

> SUSAN: You're now a Salvadoran citizen, is that right?
> GREG: As far as I know, I'm sure that's what they consider me, but now there is someone, which is really ironic, from Ohio who was adopted from Brazil. And INS [the Immigration and Naturalization Service], they, the judge signed the papers for him to be deported, but Brazil would not accept him. Because they say that his adoption was irrevocable. "You took him from here. He is now a citizen of your country." So in reality, he has no country. So I don't know how different, I don't know how they look at me here. But my friends here consider me from the United States. They consider me a citizen.
> SUSAN: Your friends here (in El Salvador) consider you a (US) citizen?
> GREG: Is it wrong that I don't explain the situation? That's my question.

Describing his efforts to reassemble his life after being sent back to El Salvador, Greg said:

> It's like trying to put a puzzle together when you don't have the pieces. It's tough. I can put the corner pieces together and some of the outside pieces, but I can't do the rest because I don't know. . . . It's very defeating. It's sort of like trying to climb up a glass mountain. You can get up a little, but shoo! You go right back down. And I never thought I'd ever say I'd rather be homeless in the United States. . . . But I firmly believe, I would rather be in prison or homeless in the United States.

Deportation from the United States reconnected Greg to a de facto legal self that had been rendered immaterial through his adoption to the United States almost two decades earlier. Adoption, in turn, created a self and a life in the United States that were forbidden to him and that haunted him in El Salvador. The disjuncture between these "immaterial corporalities" (created first by adoption and then by deportation) contributed to Greg's sense of alienage in his native land and his longing for return to the United States, his adopted country, where deportation had legally configured him as an alien.[49] Greg's experience recalls our discussion in chapter 2 of Araceli's double consciousness of being "technically" from El Salvador but feeling that LA was her home. Both deportees and immigrants who are in the United States can experience the disorientation of multiple belongings, not all of which are recognized. Greg's experience as adopted and then deported illuminates the dependence of any point of origin or of any journey "back" on the power of law to situate (and resituate) the legal subject— that is, to define (and erase) origins, the selves who originate, and the availability of a place or past to which to return. But his experience also suggests the ways that desire for a return may confound the definitions of belonging and the accompanying cutoffs authorized by law. As doubly deported, Greg may "in reality, [have] no country." At the same time, the "back" for which he longs and that continues "in reality" to compel him is not simply an effect of law's exclusionary power. Rather, this "back" has taken shape (like the person known as Greg) in the "indirect, crosswise, and crablike" movements through which Greg's sense of his past is created.[50] The path that ought to connect these persons and places is unclear, has gaps, and may not really be a path at all. From one point on this path, other points can be seen, but dimly, as when peering through translucent glass. If time were linear, this path would be transparent.[51] However, when individuals move along this path, they move *across* as well as *through* time. Time becomes a dimension of space and thus assumes a planar as well as a linear form.

Traveling such a temporal path entails multidirectional movements, not simply from present to past or future but also from one present to another. When Greg was sent "back" to El Salvador, for example, he had to become a self (a Salvadoran citizen) that he presumably (but unbeknownst to him) had been all along. Greg therefore occupied multiple locations simultaneously, but pace Greene, a different outcome singled out a different preceding history.[52] Greg's experience returns us to the paradox that adoption retroactively erases the legal birth of a child by so-called natural parents and at the same time requires such parents in order to anchor the law in a "natural" real: that is, in something that is neither here nor there but in an elsewhere, a potential space outside the law.[53] In Greg's adoption story, there should be no "back" because, officially, the back to which he could return has been erased by law. If a "back" is constituted as a function of multiple cutoffs, emigrations, and deportations, it becomes more like a network of referents than a journey with a clear end point (or a clear point of origin).[54] Just as one seems to reach that which comes before, there is a "false beginning" "right there, hitting you, slapping you in the face" (to quote another Salvadoran deportee). As Latour argues, it is only when a network of transformations ceases to refer (when its expansion is interrupted at either end, when the end point of a "back" is reached, when a true self is found) that it "begins to lie."[55]

Another example of law's power to situate and resituate the legal subject, and of how an excluded previous history may pull this subject across time into a present that has been there all along, is provided by Deann Borshay Liem's autoethnographic film, *First Person Plural*.[56] The film describes what is in effect a deportation of an eight-year-old Korean child, Kang Ok Jin, whose mother had placed her in an orphanage near her home during a period when she was unable to provide for all four of her children. One day, Kang Ok Jin is placed on a plane bound for California, accompanied by documents that provide her with a new name (Cha Jung Hee) and a new history as an orphan whose mother died and whose father relinquished her for adoption. (The 1993 Hague Convention on Intercountry Adoption requires that all children placed overseas for adoption must be declared "legal orphans" before an adoption can take place.) Liem recalls her effort, once she was able to communicate in English, to explain to her new mother that she was not an orphan, had a mother and siblings in Korea, and had a Korean name that differed from that in her adoption records. Her mother's response was that this "other family" was something Liem had dreamt, and she showed Liem the adoption records confirming her birth mother's death. Told that she just needs time to adjust to the new situation, Liem eventually forgets what she had previously known and becomes to all intents and purposes what she describes as a typical American girl.

In many ways, Liem's documentary resembles science fiction. Relocated suddenly to a new world, she is presented on her arrival with new parents, a new brother and sister, a new home, and a new language. Eventually, she fashions a new self, using makeup, surgery (her ears are operated on), and other techniques of self-fashioning. In pictures taken of her in high school, it is hard to distinguish her from other (non-Korean) teenagers in her class. It is only in her dreams that a previous reality makes itself known. When she eventually returns to Korea in hopes of recovering the family she lost and, by bringing her two families together, making herself whole, she discovers that the legal transformation of her relationship to her Korean family (and specifically to her Korean mother) was not simply a matter of law. The adoption decree transformed the existential reality of her relationship with the person she imagined to be her mother into a relationship with her not-mother, and Liem's film documents the materialization of this alternative reality: only when she realizes that her Korean mother is no longer her mother is she able to "return" to a relationship with her Korean mother as not-a-daughter, which (unbeknownst to her) had existed all along.

First Person Plural illuminates the ways that legal judgments frame and recon-stitute historical realities: Kang Ok Jin, born on June 14, 1957, becomes Cha Jung Hee, born on November 5, 1956; Cha Jung Hee becomes Deann Borshay, who was born "the moment I stepped off the plane in San Francisco on March 3, 1966."[57] Liem deploys the technologies of video and psychiatry to provide glimpses into alternative realities that fragment the time of law, tugging at the completeness of the families it creates. In the film, the legal truths of adoption and the families it completes evoke the (half) hidden truths of abandonment and the families it de-stroys. At the same time, the film documents the (half) hidden truths that pull on the ethnographer (Liem) who is at the center of the tale, as she attempts to sort out the noise (the emotional tensions with her adoptive parents, her conviction that "something was wrong") from the information she was provided (the adoption record that legitimized her identity as Cha Jung Hee). In the process, Liem oscil-lates between multiple versions of the self and between one family and another, even as the space where she is located shifts between field and not-field. Moving between impossible realities, between that which must be real and that which can-not be real, is both emotionally wrenching and enormously productive.

Analogic Thinking

In 1988, as part of my fieldwork among Tucson and Berkeley religious workers who were providing "sanctuary" to Salvadoran and Guatemalan refugees, I volunteered with TECLA, the Tucson Ecumenical Council of Legal Assistance. One day, while searching for secondary documents to support an asylum claim, I described my research to a U.S. volunteer and a Central American paralegal. "Do you remember when you were being a refugee?" the volunteer asked the paralegal. "Oh yes," he replied. "People used to look at me and say, 'You have two legs just like white people and you walk just like white people.'"

Ethnographic note, Susan Coutin

In the vignette described in the epigraph, the Central American paralegal suggests that "being a refugee" involved assuming an imposed and racialized identity, given North American sanctuary workers' preconceptions about refugees. In a similar way, Coutin and others were doing legal research in order to help Central Americans win political asylum and thus be retroactively defined as refugees. This work was necessary because of participants' presumption that

Central Americans were already de facto refugees but lacked legal recognition as such. Through advocacy and legal research (documenting claims), the law was to be brought into accordance with a social reality—the claim that a particular individual was persecuted—which also existed as a potential legal reality. Coutin's work as an ethnographer participated in this broader chain of documentation. By narrating this anecdote, her work questioned categories such as "refugee" even as her volunteer work of documenting asylum claims reproduced such categories. Relatedly noting that "sometimes it is assumed that the anthropologist is making claims to know 'more' than those he or she works with," Strathern argues that while few practicing fieldworkers would make such a claim, and while some reframe such claims as a matter of "knowing differently" rather than "more," both of these characterizations miss an important point: that "the anthropologist is equally trying to know in the *same* way—that is, recover some of the anticipation of fieldwork, some of the revelations that came from the personal relationships established there, and even perhaps some of the surprises which people keep in store for one another."[58]

This revelation, that being an anthropologist is an effect of succumbing to a legal (or other) process analogous to that through which refugees, deportees, or adoptees are produced, points both to the limits and to the potentials of ethnographic knowledge. Our understanding of adoption as contingent on a deportation that necessarily precedes it—or, to put it another way, that a deportation is framed as an adoption, cutting off the forms of exclusion that made the child adoptable—can be seen as an ethnographic effect: the effect of being dazzled by, and thus yielding ourselves to, the potentialities of data we each had collected that kept pulling us back to fields. In the process of this return, we found ourselves repeatedly up against the slim thread (and vast gulf) that separates deportations and roots trips, and the position of the ethnographer in the middle of the relational field in which each takes shape vis-à-vis the other.

Being in the middle situates ethnographers at a key juncture in the evaluation of truth. Ethnographic truth no more resides in the "face-to-face confrontation of a mind with an object" than does the value of a "thing" referred to by a term of reference in a sentence reside in its physical verification as an object in the world.[59] Rather, truth value "passes across" ethnographers, whose questions when they enter the field are deflected by a mass of data that is way more than they can possibly write down—and that continues to dazzle them upon leaving the field.[60] The "longing for correspondence" that pulls anthropologists into the thick of things in a field (of events, of notes), where at times there seems to be only noise, produces the conditions for this movement of truth value: ethnographers continually bump up against the ephemeral quality of realities that remain (half) hidden, always demanding just one more journey back.[61]

This process of circulation (of ethnographers through the field, of value across ethnographers) is only cut in the process of producing a good (an article for publication, a film),[62] a form of reification or objectification that works to make value visible in another form (the deportation that was half hidden within the adoption; Greg's experience of becoming a Salvadoran self that, unbeknownst to him, he had been all along). These forms may, in turn, disrupt the obvious correspondences that pull people back to supposedly original (natural, national) grounds of belonging that are authorized by law.

The activism of transnational adoptees over the past two decades provides one approach to such forms of disruption, notably in regular international gatherings of Korean-born adoptees that have become a movable ground for a deterritorialized community that is active on the Internet, in publications, in films, in art installations, and in face-to-face meetings around the world. In these and other venues, adoptees produce alternative accounts of belonging and invent new forms of value that implicitly challenge conventions that allow giving and receiving nations to determine where and to whom the adoptees really belong.[63] Similarly, immigrant rights activists have sought to challenge the accountings that result in deportations, and deportees have argued that they deserve recognition as "the other dreamers," the counterparts of immigrant youth in the United States.[64] In both of these cases, the task of the ethnographer (like Benjamin's translator) is to "engage what information [she] has with limited expertise and an enduring sense" of the tragedies in which her work is embedded.[65] At times inundated with data, ethnographers' only hope is to seek further entanglements.

Such entanglement is depicted in the short story "Schrödinger's Cat," written by Ursula K. Le Guin, science fiction novelist and daughter of the famous anthropologist Alfred Kroeber, a contemporary of Schrödinger and founder of the Department of Anthropology at the University of California, Berkeley.[66] In Le Guin's version, the narrator, who has found a stray cat, is approached by a dog carrying a box, the very box that is set up to carry out Schrödinger's thought experiment. The dog insists that the narrator place the cat in the box. Before the narrator can refuse, the cat leaps into the box, knocking the lid shut. In search of certainty, the dog waits for the narrator to open the box. The narrator does so, and

> Rover staggered up from his knees, gasping, to look. The cat was, of course, not there. Rover neither barked, nor fainted, nor cursed, nor wept. He really took it very well. "Where is the cat?" he asked at last.
> "Where is the box?"
> "Here."
> "Where's here?"
> "Here is now."

"We used to think so," I said, "but really we should use larger boxes."

He gazed about him in mute bewilderment, and did not flinch even when the roof of the house was lifted off just like the lid of a box, letting in the unconscionable, inordinate light of the stars. He had just time to breathe. "Oh, wow!"[67]

THE SEARCH FOR A "BACK"

Archivists of Memory

Searching for solutions is very much part of a struggle to survive. The concept of "searching" is embedded in our [Maori and indigenous] world views. . . . Research . . . begins with human curiosity and a desire to solve problems. It is at its core an activity of hope.

Smith, *Decolonizing Methodologies*

In this chapter, we consider the *estado de búsqueda* ("state of searching," "quest") that materializes within several sorts of returns: roots trips that adoptees take to the places where they were born; searches that relatives of the disappeared conduct for their loved ones; exiles' quest to understand the past, even as it erupts in the present; and ethnographers' returns (via fieldnotes) to their field sites. In each of these cases, there is a powerful pull to a "back," which may be intensified by the tension between the longing for a time and space before the present, and the impossibility of fully reaching such a point. When the pull is to a position that was legally recorded or erased, returns may be focused on a search for papers. Papers literally enliven and extinguish persons in their search for or abduction from particular realities. Papers may be unavailable, because in cases of deportation, adoption, or other forms of social dislocation, documents may be sealed, destroyed, or altered to cancel an extant juridical person or produce a new juridical self. Moreover, the search for documents may be complicated by the possibility that papers—birth certificates, passports, court records, secret files, fieldnotes—that provoke movement and authenticate identity can assume multiple and contradictory forms. The lack or proliferation of these forms produces tensions between papers (which should authenticate a self that preexists its documentation) and the experience of a self that papers can never fully represent. Adoption, for example, is haunted by the canceled persona (the establishment of legal abandonment or orphan status) that preceded it, and deportation likewise is haunted by the potential that legal adoption (i.e., an award of citizenship) might have provided, as suggested in the adoption and deportation narratives of Greg and Deann Borshay Liem in chapter 3.

The necessity yet impossibility of return gives rise to a paradox: access to an evidentiary record—to the time and space before death, deportation, adoption, or departure—holds out the promise of wholeness but also the risk of annihilation as the world that one imagined or experienced is undone.[1] Temporally and spatially, this undoing is akin to Winnicott's "continuity-contiguity moment": a time and space in which a fundamental break in the continuity of being gives way to "new possibilities of relationships between worlds."[2] An example of the way such a break may give rise to new possibilities of relationship is provided in Patricio Guzmán's powerful 2010 documentary, *Nostalgia for the Light*. The documentary follows Chilean women searching for the remains of loved ones who were disappeared during the 1973–90 dictatorship of Augusto Pinochet in Chile. The women describe finding fragments of the bodies of brothers, sons, or husbands in Chile's Atacama Desert after Pinochet's overthrow. The bodies had been buried in mass graves but were disinterred and scattered throughout the desert or over the ocean in order to hide traces of the government's actions, in effect producing a second disappearance to cover the first. The women are shown searching in the desert, alone or in groups of two, three, or more. An archaeologist involved in excavating the remains asks one of the searchers, a woman named Vicky, "What did you find of your brother, finally?"[3] She responds:

> A foot, his foot inside a shoe; part of his denture, part of his nose and forehead—the left part of his head. The back part of his ear with a hole where the shot came through and the shattered forehead where they gave the final coup de grace. I remembered his loving expression, and this was all that was left. I knew it was his foot. A smell of decomposition, a burgundy sock. I took it home with me that night in a bag. The next day, I took it out of the bag and contemplated it. My husband went to work. I remained sitting with the foot—my mind was a blank. We were reunited. Only in that moment did I understand that my brother was dead.

Winnicott describes experiences such as Vicky's in the intermediate zone between psychic, or internal, reality and shared, or exterior, reality as "akin to dream-work" or "mystical experiences."[4] His research in this area concerned "the substance of *illusion*, that which is allowed to the infant, and which in adult life is inherent in art and religion, and yet becomes the hallmark of madness when an adult puts too powerful a claim on the credulity of others, forcing them to acknowledge a sharing of illusion that is not their own."[5] As another woman searching for remains of a loved one in the Atacama explained in response to the question, "Will you carry on searching?":

> While I can, I will. But I have lots of doubts, lots of questions. What if they threw them in the sea, or on top of the mountain [gesturing to the mountains rising from the desert floor]? At this point in my life, I am seventy and it is hard for me to believe things [*me cuesta creer cosas*]. They taught me to believe. It's hard for me—sometimes I am seen as stupid, because I pose questions, questions, questions and at the end no one can give me the answer I want. . . . They tell me there are fewer and fewer of the women. Fewer problems. Because we are a problem— for society, for justice, for everyone. We were regarded as the lowest of the low. Like the lepers of Chile. That's what I think.

A second example of how circling back in search of more information about the disappearance of a lost object may open up new possibilities of relationships between worlds is provided by the experience of Sofia Berzelius, whom Barbara first met in Stockholm in 1998. Berzelius, who was adopted from Ethiopia as an infant and whose experience of double consciousness in Sweden after her first trip back to Addis Ababa in her thirties was described in chapter 2, made that journey back in hopes of finding more information about her birth mother's death in childbirth and her own abandonment. She had been told in Sweden that there were no details about her origins, since St. Paul's Hospital, where she was born, was for the very poor: "People who died there were just put outside and were just picked up by some truck in the morning and dumped somewhere. When I heard that I was sort of sad, because I would have wished to—Oh! Well! So that was about all I knew when I went there."[6] But on her arrival in Addis Ababa, Berzelius discovered the Amharic original of her birth certificate at the records office and, with the help of a translator, confirmed that her mother had died from complications related to the delivery; but the translator also discovered "an extra sentence" in the Amharic version that had been "dropped out" of the English translation. The sentence stated that the grandmother of the baby was present at the delivery and "was asked if she would take care of the child," but she declined to do so. Sofia also discovered that, contrary to the information she had received in Sweden, St. Paul's Hospital, where she was born, was still standing. Offered a tour of the hospital, she was taken through the maternity ward and eventually to the operating theater, where she had been delivered: "And there was this really, really amazing feeling, because suddenly I just touched ground. It was fantastic just to see. It was like, 'Yeah, OK, so this is where it started.'"

Sister Danielle, the midwife who served as her guide at the hospital, offered to look up the record of Sofia's birth in the hospital files. Sofia was amazed to discover that this hospital that supposedly "didn't exist" not only existed but also had well-organized files, and that "for every day, they had made little, little records." Sofia explained,

> This was not according to my picture of Ethiopia. To me, Ethiopia would be just chaos. But there, it was written that on the date when I was born, there were thirteen deliveries, and I had a paper where my birth weight was written down, so we found me. We found my biological mother's name. And it turns out that she had actually been coming for regular check-ups. This was her second delivery, and she was twenty-six years old. She had died from a hemorrhage. We could see what time of the day I was born and how long I was and what the name of the doctor was.

She continued: "It was *so* different from what I expected. It just felt good for me to find out that this place that I had heard about and the stories that I had heard about this country and the place where I was born were so wrong. The people who worked there were so kind and they were so helpful. It was just so nice to find out that this is where I was born, this is where I come from."

In this account of going back, there is a constant undercurrent of tension: between papers and stories, between Amharic and English, between the elation of discovering "where I come from" and "where it started," and the reality of abandonment in Sofia's grandmother's refusal to care for her. Sofia explained her decision not to follow up on what she had learned about her mother's name and the presence of her grandmother at her birth:

> I just felt it was too much already. Also I figured there must have been some reasons for this grandmother not to want to take care of me, so I thought I needed to think about this. For instance, if I would find out who they are and if I would find out that they are extremely poor, what would I do with that? Do I have any obligations? Do I want to have those obligations? Can I handle it? What does it mean? Is it important? So therefore I haven't followed up on it, but I might.

For people who are adopted or deported, as for relatives of the disappeared in Chile, records of the presence of a lost object—including but not limited to papers—become key transitional phenomena, testifying to the violent reality surrounding a political or legal disappearance, even as they materialize a kind of presence that anchors the searcher's continuity of being. As a result, paper and other evidentiary trails do not merely document prior moments and movements but also have the potential to redefine persons, compel movement, alter moments, and make ties ambiguous. Instead of only trailing into the past, papers jut out into the future, requiring the selves who are authenticated by these documents to chart new and sometimes unanticipated courses.

A State of Searching

Sofia's return to Ethiopia and Vicky's recovery of her brother's foot point to the powerful pull exerted by an adoption, deportation, or abduction as disappearances continue to haunt the selves who carry on. For both Sofia and Vicky, carrying on meant entering what an archaeologist interviewed in *Nostalgia for the Light* refers to as a "state of searching": "Pero olvidar una tragedia de esa naturaleza, eso no es posible. Hay que vivir en estado de búsqueda." (But to forget a tragedy of this nature, that is not possible. One must live in a state of searching.) Living in an *estado de búsqueda* is like hovering on the edge of a breach between presence and absence or life and death. To an extent, negotiating this breach is a dimension of all human experience.[7] It requires, as we have suggested in our discussion of Winnicott, "the use of illusion, without which there is no meaning for the human being in the idea of a relationship with an object that is perceived by others as external to that being."[8]

In the *estado de búsqueda* that we discuss here, the stakes of a search are heightened due to the tension between two forces. One is the *form of existence*, which is legitimized on the basis of multiple forms of disappearance. Such disappearances include illicit abductions and the presumed killings that followed, which were seemingly intended to legitimize the political order; legal "abandonments" that are required by law and that underpin adoptions; and forced deportations that supposedly legitimize national sovereignty. The second force is the *technologies of forgetting*, which are instantiated to erase memories of these disappearances.[9] Thus, the state of searching referred to by the archaeologist in *Nostalgia for the Light* requires a heightened "state of attention" in which grasping "the past" requires "seiz[ing] hold of a memory as it flashes up at a moment of danger. . . . Only that historian will have the gift of fanning the spark of hope in the past who is firmly convinced that *even the dead* will not be safe from the enemy if he wins."[10]

Here we discuss states of searching initiated in response to a diverse range of disappearances. These states materialize in such locations as the Atacama Desert in Chile, and the universe made visible there through the work of optical and radio astronomy researchers; the abysses of Abu Salim prison in Libya; abandoned police archives in Guatemala; and the memories of survivors. As searchers struggle to remain there, between absence and presence, a transitional space where past and future intermingle, they locate traces of the realities to which they seek access.

These traces may take the form of bone fragments, pieces of cloth, records, a map, images, memories, or testimony. In gathering such remains, those who search also bring light to the darkness surrounding disappearances, as Samuele's flashlight lit the tree branches where he sought a baby bird (see chapter 2) or as Rover discovered when the lid was taken off the house (see chapter 3) or as astronomers' telescopes in the Atacama Desert allow light to flood in.[11]

Papers play complex roles within searchers' efforts to connect to the past. For example, *Nostalgia for the Light* recounts the experiences of Miguel, described as an "architect of memory" who, under Pinochet, was imprisoned in five of Pinochet's concentration camps, including Chacabuco, the largest of these. Repurposed from dwellings occupied by nineteenth-century miners who lived in the desert, Chacabuco was occupied by those who had been clandestinely abducted by the Chilean government between November 1973 and October 1974, and then was subsequently destroyed by the military. The film depicts Miguel walking with measured footsteps to show how he kept track of the configuration of the prison camp: "I decided to leave a testimony. Each day I walked, and discreetly measured rooms so I could later testify [if I survived]." While imprisoned, Miguel made drawings of the camp by candlelight, perhaps on toilet paper; then he memorized them, tore them up, and threw them into the latrine. When he was released after Pinochet's overthrow, Miguel reconstructed these plans and made them public, leaving the military, which had thought it could avoid discovery, "dumbstruck." The destroyed papers can be seen as a form of transitional object, connecting Miguel's measurements while in the camp to his later efforts to counter the denial that the place had existed. By reproducing plans that had been engraved in his mind, Miguel brought the time and space of disappearances to light, enabling his testimony to circulate in the world of things, where it could have legal effect. Here, Miguel's training as an architect and his lived experience in the camps made possible a kind of archiving of the layout of Pinochet's concentration camps, a process in which both embodied skill and conscious determination to survive were involved. While acknowledging the vast difference in each situation, we suggest that there is a way in which Miguel and Gianfranco Rosi, the documentary filmmaker who made the film about Lampedusa and the circumstances of migrants there (*Fire at Sea*, discussed in chapter 2), can be said to have worked in analogous ways in making visible clandestine or generally invisible processes in the prison camp in the Atacama Desert and the migrant holding center on Lampedusa. In each case, a place becomes a kind of "mental map" from which the architect who came to know Chacabuco through torture, forced labor, and prison routines, and the filmmaker who sought to grasp the enemy on Lampedusa through the games of a child and the chanting of migrants, were able to "grab and grasp the truth that belonged so intimately to each" place, a truth that was hidden in the bodies and memories of those who were caught up in the histories of violence that played out there.[12]

Another example of the effort to traverse the gulf between imprisonment and release (or imprisonment and death) occurs in Hisham Matar's 2016 memoir, *The Return*, which recounts Matar's quest to learn the fate of his father, Jaballa Matar, who was abducted in Cairo in 1990 and never seen again. Other members of Jaballa's extended family who were imprisoned at the same time he was abducted eventually confirmed that he was taken to Qaddafi's infamous Abu Salim prison in Tripoli, where he was held until at least 1996, when a rebellion among the prisoners led to a massacre of some twelve hundred men. On the eve of Qaddafi's overthrow in 2011, Jaballa's relatives, who had by then been in prison for over twenty years, were released, along with others, as a way of attempting to appease the growing resistance to Qaddafi. There was no word of the fate of Jaballa, however. At the heart of the memoir is Hisham's journey back to Libya in 2012 with his mother and his wife, Diana, for the first time in the more than thirty years since his family fled the country in the mid-1970s. After lunch in his grandfather's ancestral home in Ajdabiya, Matar sat with his Uncle Mahmoud, who had been imprisoned. Matar says that his uncle's stories about imprisonment

> were aimed at proving that the authorities had failed, that he [Matar's uncle] had not been erased, that he continued to remember and even managed to follow, through the radio the guards occasionally allowed him, what his nephew the novelist [Matar himself] was up to in faraway London. *His stories were an attempt to bridge the vast distance that separated the austere cruelty of Abu Salim and the world outside.* Perhaps, like all stories, what Uncle Mahmoud's recollections were saying was: 'I exist.'"[13]

Just as Miguel's reconstructed architectural plans proved the existence of Chacabuco, so too did Matar's uncle's stories reassert his own existence, his refusal to be erased, and his reclaiming of a self who was someone other than what the authorities believed him to be.

These examples suggest that returning to the past, whether by reconstructing the architecture of a clandestine concentration camp or by narrating experiences of imprisonment, excavates and thus intervenes in the future. Returns move forward as well as backward in time, a point that is explicit in the film *Nostalgia for the Light*, as astronomers, archaeologists, and relatives of the disappeared search in the Atacama Desert for the origins of the universe, artifacts of prehistoric humans, and the remains of the disappeared. The lack of moisture in the Atacama made the atmosphere so transparent that powerful telescopes could capture the ancient light of distant stars, while the dry, sandy soil preserved artifacts that might otherwise decay. Even though Pinochet's takeover made it difficult for Chilean researchers to continue their work, the Atacama remained a key research center for foreign scholars, and despite Pinochet's efforts to raze his prison camp and scatter the remains of the disappeared, the Atacama also became a place where traces of those who disappeared during the Pinochet period could be recovered. One of the archaeologists interviewed in the film observes that these searches are interconnected: "The astronomers have made a huge telescope to bring together [pause] the origins of everything and the past of the past of everything. They are in the present receiving and reconstructing the past. They are as much archaeologists as we are." In fact, as a narrator points out, the calcium in the bone fragments uncovered by both archaeologists and relatives of the disappeared is a key element in the stars studied by astronomers. Thus, astronomy is an archaeology of the heavens and archaeology is an astronomy of the earth. In the words of a young astronomer whose parents were killed during Pinochet's rule, together, these disciplines can document a cycle that "neither began nor ended in me, nor my parents, nor my children, but we are all part of . . . an energy of recyclable matter, as with the stars. They have to die so that there can be other stars, planets, life. And in this game (*en ese juego*), I think that what happened to them and their absence takes on another dimension, a new meaning, and it frees me from the pain and great hurt, the feeling that when things end, they end."[14]

The multidirectional temporality of the *estado de búsqueda* is also evident within accounts of exile and return. Hisham Matar, for example, describes experiencing a sort of temporal disruption when returning to his childhood room in Cairo in 2012, the night before he flew to Libya to search for his father: "I was now fifteen. I was now 41. I was now eight."[15] Revisiting places from a time before, as part of an effort to produce a different future, produces something of a temporal instability. Shahram Khosravi's autoethnography *"Illegal" Traveller*, which recounts his own flight from Iran; travels through Afganistan, Pakistan, and India; and exile in Sweden, describes a similar sensation: "Exilic life is the constant presence of the absent."[16] Khosravi finds that he can be engaged in everyday activities, like eating in a coffee shop or writing on the board in class, when suddenly images of his life in Iran appear in his mind, "Like a slide show." He explains, "They are an interruption in the rhythm of the present, an intermezzo. In exile, one does not stand on firm ground. Exile is a condition of transience. . . . Exile is only parenthetic to life, though it lasts and lasts, though I know return is only a myth, a never-to-be-realized dream, though I know there is no home to go back to."[17] Though disruptive, such temporal movements, in which the past erupts in the present or an individual re-experiences prior moments, enable a kind of connection. In this sense, the *estado de búsqueda* also shares features of an archive. As Derrida has noted, archives safeguard the past in anticipation of the future and are therefore forward-looking.[18] Furthermore, documents that record past events have what Eric Ketelaar describes as a "membranic" quality in that they allow "the infusing and exhaling of values which are embedded in each and every activation."[19]

Migrants, adoptees, and relatives of the disappeared are not the only ones who seek to record the past; state agents who are responsible for disappearances and who create conditions that propel migration or make babies adoptable create their own archives. In contrast to the lack of information faced by those in an *estado de búsqueda*, state agents may have an abundance of documentation, even if it is not publicly accessible. This was the case in Guatemala, where multiple archives document the mechanisms of terror during that country's thirty-six years of civil war. These include "adoption archives" that "conjure up" ubiquitous accounts of disappearing children during this period, suggesting the continuities between an extrajudicial system that regulated transnational adoption and the Guatemalan National Police's clandestine archives, discovered by accident by human rights activists in a warehouse where millions of records were bundled together, crumbling, becoming moldy, eaten by worms, and used by vermin as nests.[20] Kristen Weld, who chronicled the effort to rescue this archive and make it usable, writes that the police kept these potentially incriminating documents because without them, police could not do their work: "Crudely put, in order to kill university students or community organizers, one had to keep track of who they were, who their friends and relatives were, and what daily routes they traveled. . . . The police records, which compiled these very types of intelligence information, [were important] to the 'successful' execution of the counterinsurgency."[21] The time before disappearance was therefore also a time of surveillance. For example, police files were kept on Guatemalan politician Manuel Colom Argueta for twenty-two years before the police assassinated him.[22] Weld describes how police activities instigated the *estado de búsqueda* that relatives experienced after their loved ones disappeared: "Plainclothes *hombres desconocidos* . . . with a few moments' scuffle and a plateless Ford Bronco, set parents, lovers, siblings, and children on long and desperate searches for, to borrow Carlos Figueroa Ibarra's phrase, 'los que siempre estarán en ninguna parte' (those who will always be nowhere)."[23] *Ninguna parte* (nowhere) is, in a sense, the half-hidden counterpart of the places where those who search were located. In the archives, searchers sometimes reencountered records of disappeared persons they knew, bringing these moments together and leading the searchers to relive the past, but from the perspective of the police. As Weld writes, "Reencountering the war through the Other's eyes blurred comfortable distinctions between present and past, memory and history."[24]

As they move through time, blurring boundaries between memory and history, papers and other materializations of a disappeared reality connect the empty space of disappearances to a present "state of searching" in which survivors and other activists are immersed. There is a connection, then, between the *estado de búsqueda* and the continuity/contiguity moment that it opens up in the aftermath of state-instigated disappearances. Entering the *estado de búsqeda* is like entering a parallel reality, one in which the (dis)appearances of the everyday in the worlds created by Qaddafi in Libya, Pinochet in Chile, and a series of US-supported dictators in Guatemala are brought to light but in a different form. Human rights activists who worked in the Guatemalan police archives reencountered past selves as "paper cadavers," Vicky reencountered her brother when his decomposed foot was found, the architect Miguel made visible the space of disappearance recorded in his memory by drawing plans.

The *estado de búsqueda*, we suggest, is a sort of metamessage, or metalinguistic communication. As we discussed in chapter 3, Gregory Bateson argued that the metalinguistic communication "This is play," which is often implicit, sets up a paradox in that actions (such as the nip of a dog) do not convey their normal meanings (a fight) but rather the opposite (play). In Bateson's words, the message "This is play" means "These actions, in which we now engage, do not denote what would be denoted by those actions which these actions denote."[25] The *estado de búsqueda* likewise establishes a paradox: though they are internal states, memory, fear, loss, and grief can be put out into the world (for example, through the photographs that relatives of the disappeared compile) and can be reencountered in objects. Such objects potentially confirm searchers' knowledge by enabling them to access traces of the reality that, to paraphrase Khosravi, is not there to go back to. As one of the archaeologists interviewed in *Nostalgia for the Light* states, "The present doesn't exist—really," noting that when "I say 'I am me,'" there is a lapse in speaking the sentence that separates "I" from "me." "My consciousness of being me—even that has a certain delay."[26]

The delay that makes the present not exist, really, is linked to the difficulty of exiting the endless expanse of searching. To again quote an archaeologist featured in *Nostalgia for the Light*, "The translucency of the sky is to the astronomer as the dry climate is for us. That's why we share the space. . . . It is a door we know how to enter, but how will we exit?"[27] For deportees, migrants, adoptees, and relatives of the disappeared, time stretches into endless waiting, whether for asylum, news, the opportunity to return, or a reencounter.[28] Hisham Matar describes this temporal expanse as *"the condition of waiting*. It turns out that I have spent all the time since I was eight years old, when my family left Libya, waiting. My silent condemnation of those fellow exiles who wished to assimilate—which is to say, my bloody-minded commitment to rootlessness—was *my feeble act of fidelity to the old country, or maybe not even to Libya but to the young boy I was when we left.*"[29] For Matar, fidelity to place produced rootlessness, a sort of being in multiple dimensions or states of being at the same time.

Alive-Deadness

In accounts of being in an *estado de búsqueda*, we repeatedly found imagery suggesting that both persons and histories that have been rendered inaccessible through law, violence, or dislocation exist in a sort of alive-dead state, much like the cat in Schrödinger's thought experiment (see chapter 3). For example, in Guatemala, a key slogan of the families of the disappeared was, "Porque vivos se los llevaron, ¡vivos los queremos!" (Because they were taken away alive, we want them back alive!)[30] While family members knew that their relatives had most likely been killed, this refrain refused to accept disappearance as the equivalent of death, insisting instead on knowledge, accountability, and return before any determination of death could be made. Demanding that the disappeared be returned alive seeks recognition of the reality of what might otherwise seem to exist only in memory or in the imagination, namely the fact that the disappeared were living people. In the words of one of the individuals who sought to restore the archives of the Guatemalan National Police, "All of the cadavers that turn up as XX or unidentified, all of those cadavers had names. And they were killed, and things were done to them, and that was because they had names. It wasn't because they were nameless."[31] The records that allow bodies to be named externalize memory, serving as a material trace or concrete evidence of a living person. In this sense, alive-deadness resembles what Simmel describes as the paradox of value: "exchange as a means of overcoming the purely subjective value significance of an object," since it suggests value "independently of me."[32] Paradoxically, the distance between externalized and subjective forms of memory, between objects and persons, is not there (because an object can be the materialization of memory) and yet cannot be bridged (to the degree that objects and persons are different orders of being: one is alive and the other, supposedly, is not). As one archaeologist quoted in *Nostalgia for the Light* stated, "I would not be able to forget, I would have the ethical obligation to capture that memory. It is impossible to forget our dead. One must keep them in memory."[33]

As a paradoxical irresolution, alive-deadness partakes of what Kim Fortun refers to as "a juxtapositional logic, a logic wherein divergent ways of seeing (often the same thing) are brought together . . . what one gets when one sees through different analytic lenses, from different vantage points. Not to resolve differences nor to merely celebrate diversity, but to provoke encounters across difference that produce new articulations."[34] Filmmakers Guzmán and Rosi both use juxtapositions productively—for example, cutting from a mummified hand to a supernova to convey multiple ways that the past is preserved, or moving between a doctor listening to an Italian boy take deep breaths and the hold of a ship where refugees trying to reach Italy died due to lack of oxygen (see chapter 2). We have employed a juxtapositional logic in this book as well, bringing together multiple attempts to document impossible realities. In fact, memory itself can be construed as a creative form of juxtaposition. As Marie Claire Sekkel writes regarding Walter Benjamin's understanding of play and the invention of the world,

> The fabric of remembering is not a reflection of the facts, of life the way it really happened, but the game of similarities, which happens beyond what our consciousness is able to apprehend. . . . The similarity invents a coherent relationship, that does not meet the criteria of causality or functionality, which is living tissue that supports the existence. The continuity of being involves the creation of these support bridges over the unfathomable depths of the breaks in the continuity, which are felt as a threat. Human experience happens in the construction of these bridges.[35]

The juxtaposition of fragments that are beyond consciousness is the manifestation of a "creative impulse," a movement between continuity (past, present, and future) and contiguity (encountering oneself in the world).[36] The *estado de búsqueda* transcends or moves between life and death, much like the seemingly lifeless plants of the Atacama Desert can blossom suddenly when there is rain.

Alive-deadness is temporally complex. As the narrator explains in *Nostalgia for the Light*, "Memory has the force of gravity. It constantly attracts us. Those who have memory are able to live in the fragile present moment. Those who don't have it don't live anywhere." Erasures—through disappearances, adoption, migration, the denial of citizenship, or other processes—create a pull to the past, a pull that enables a present moment to form.[37] In this formulation, instead of seeing the past as *producing* the present, the present gives rise to a need for the past, creating perhaps a "double life"—the Chile of Pinochet and the earlier Chile that was "a haven of peace and democracy."[38] By refusing to abandon their search, the women in the Atacama Desert were an "irritating presence"—like the "Ethiopianness" of adoptees in Sweden (see chapter 1)—reminding others that the Chile of Pinochet had happened and could not simply be erased without accountability. Rather, it—along with the spaces created by the repression—had to be remembered. These spaces include both prison camps and the space of exile, a space that one astronomer who was interviewed describes as nowhere, saying that he is an "hijo de exilio—no soy de ninguna parte" (child of exile, I am not from any-where). Though this astronomer was born in Germany, as the child of refugees he did not feel that he was from Germany or Chile but rather from a non-space, *ninguna parte*. But "nowhere" can also bridge unfathomable breaks in continuity. Valentina, another astronomer, whose parents were disappeared when she was only a year old, was ultimately able to view "what happened to them and their absence" through both pain and optimism. Her grandparents "had the wisdom to take on a double responsibility": they enabled her to see her parents as exam-ples of idealism and bravery and also created a space for her to have happiness in her childhood. For Valentina, memory became a resource for the future.

Hisham Matar's memoir of his search for his father, abducted from Cairo and presumably killed in a prison massacre in Libya, also explores the implications of alive-deadness for his own being. Regarding his father, Matar writes, "His place is here and occupied by something that cannot just be called memory. It is alive and current. . . . My father is dead and alive. I do not have a grammar for him."[39] Though Matar's father suffered an exceptional fate, Matar sees his own effort to comprehend his father's status as akin to those of others who have lost their fathers: "He is in the past, present and future. Even if I had held his hand, and felt it slacken, as he exhaled his last breath, I would still, I believe, every time I refer to him, pause to search for the right tense. I suspect many men who have buried their fathers feel the same."[40] To Matar, his father has become something of a phantasm, a state that complicates his own being: "When a father is neither dead nor alive, when he is a ghost, the will is impotent."[41] Of the phantasm, Iser, draw-ing on Husserl, writes, "The phantasm is marked by the duality of simultaneously being present and not being taken for present; it is simultaneously something and not itself. It becomes the medium for the appearance of what is not."[42] When de-fined in relation to this phantasm, Matar himself takes on a degree of irresolution in that he experiences this duality, as though one version of himself lived in Lon-don, while another version continued living in Benghazi. When he returned to Benghazi, which he described as a "pre-life," he found that it was

> like catching your reflection in a public place. Your first reaction, before you realize it is you, is suspicion. You lose your footing but just in time regain your balance. I realize now that my walks, whether taken to pass the time or to better acquaint myself with a foreign city, or conducted in a hurry—to post a letter, to catch a train or on the occasion I was late for an appointment—all took place under the vague suspicion that I might somehow come upon myself, that is to say, that other self who lives in harmony with his surroundings, who exists, like a chapter in a book, in the right place, not torn out and left to make sense on its own.[43]

This state of irresolution, though disorienting, enables Matar to perceive reality differently. He is within and outside reality at the same time, which allows "this very world to be perceived from a vantage point that has never been part of it."[44] For example, Matar had a habit of repeatedly visiting the National Gallery in London, where he would gaze at a particular painting for fifteen minutes and do this for several days a week. After a week or sometimes months or years, he would switch to a different painting. Years later, when he learned that his father most likely died on June 29, 1996, during a massacre at Abu Salim, Matar reviewed his diary from 1996, where he discovered that on June 29, the very day that unbeknownst to him his father had died, his attention in the National Gallery had switched to Édouard Manet's *The Execution of Maximilian*, an image that he also chose for the cover of his memoir. Matar notes that large chunks of Manet's painting remain missing, and that "you cannot see Maximilian—only his hand, gripped tightly by one of his generals. The firing squad is as ruthlessly focused and indifferent as the men surrounding Saint Lawrence. It would be hard to think of a painting that better evokes the inconclusive fate of my father and the men who died in Abu Salim."[45]

Perceiving reality differently can also entail temporal juxtapositions and displacements, as Matar experienced when, during his return to Benghazi, he read a short story that his father had published as a young man. To his surprise, the story ended with the sentence, "I decided to work and survive," a phrasing that echoed an admonition, "Work and survive," that Matar associated with his father and that had repeatedly helped him cope with challenges. Matar related:

> Running into that familiar call, which has long represented my rescue, and finding it in the shape of the closing sentence of one of only two short stories my father ever published, was oddly consoling and disquieting. *It flipped time on its head.* The words were not coming to me from a parental authority now but through the eighteen-year-old who was yet to become my father, a man young enough to be my son, a talented and ambitious student who might have sought out my thoughts about becoming a writer. . . . *The stories were a profound discovery. They were a gift sent back through time, opening a window onto the interior landscape of the young man who was to become my father.* They were forward-looking, interested in finding a contemporary mode in which to write about Libya, but they were also engaged in the past.[46]

This experience recalls Gregory Bateson's discussion of double vision (Matar encounters externally a saying that he had internalized) and abduction (Matar is pulled to the voice of his eighteen-year-old father, which resonates with the voice that had been inside his head).[47] Through this abduction, Matar moves through time, meeting (in a sense) a younger version of his father while also realizing that through the story, his father also hoped to shape the future. This temporal movement enables Matar to see different moments in his father's life simultaneously; yet, Matar's effort to go back to a time before is risky, because if one reaches an origin point, one may be lost.[48] Matar recognizes this risk when he worries that if he actually were to visit the prison Abu Salim, "that place where his [Matar's father's] smell, and times, and spirit lingered (for they must linger), I might be forever undone."[49] Thus, not only persons but also the "prior existence" that is the target of a search have an alive-dead quality.

Shahram Khosravi's account of his life in exile from Iran eloquently conveys the duality of alive-deadness:

> According to an old Afghan legend, the soul leaves the body when one dreams. If one wakes up before one's soul has returned to the body, one enters an eternal nightmare (*kabous*), an outlandish predicament. For me this is what exile is about: my soul did not return in time. Exile is when you live in one place and dream in another. Exile is a dream of going back home. In exile, one is possessed by longing, no matter where the exile takes place. The whole world becomes a prison. . . . A life in exile is like being condemned to purgatory, a state between life and death, a limbo between here and there. Like many others in exile, I have an ambivalent relationship with space and time. My body is physically here and now while my heart is there and then. The spatial dimension of exilic life is *excluding, vicious and wounding*. In allocating the social spaces, the exiles are not counted.[50]

This passage powerfully conveys the existential separation entailed in alive-deadness, the gravitational pull of the longed-for back, and the location of exiles in *ninguna parte*, the non-space where one is not counted. There are connections between the space of Abu Salim where Matar's father was likely assassinated, the Chilean concentration camp where Miguel recorded and then destroyed architectural plans, and the space of exile occupied by Khosravi. These spaces have a phantasmagoric quality in that they are there even as their existence may be denied, erased, or defined as something else. Khosravi captures this spatial irresolution when he observes that "exilic life is the constant presence of the absent."[51] Exiles are in two places at once, even as they are nowhere, in *ninguna parte*.

Khosravi's recollection of his departure describes how entering exile tears space apart, creating the realm of unreality, of nowhere: "I left my *home*. I knew that the tranquil street soon would be filled with children on their way to school and their parents to their jobs. The old lady in the house across from us would go, large bag in hand, on her daily tour to the fruit and vegetable bazaar, and vendors' voices would disturb those still in bed. . . . That morning was, for others, just like any other morning. For me, the sorrow was excruciating. After two decades, memory of that morning still evokes enormous pain."[52] This account juxtaposes the ordinariness of daily life with the extraordinariness of the time and space that Khosravi was entering. For Khosravi, the tranquil street had already become distant. He could not be one of the people in bed hearing vendors' voices, he would not see the old lady across the street. Already, Khosravi was located elsewhere, even though he was still there and was about to leave. And, seemingly, he continued to see this scene in his memory, from his vantage point in exile, just as homelands occupy important imaginative space for migrants, deportees, and transnational adoptees.

The multidimensionality of alive-dead spaces is also evident in Kirsten Weld's account of the recovery of the Guatemalan National Police archives in the early 2000s. Found in 2005 by accident, after repeated requests for information about the disappeared met with state insistence that no records existed, these moldering archives were in a state of disarray, discarded like trash yet also not destroyed, in case the police themselves had need of them. To recuperate these documents, archive workers spent months in

> *la isla*, as it was called in the 1980s when the police used it to detain and torture dissidents. One area of the site in particular, the prison-like *laberinto* (labyrinth) . . . was especially difficult to handle with its windowless, dirt-floored rooms, suspicious small holes blasted in the walls, and sections fitted with what appeared to be brackets for manacles or other bindings. "Entering that space gives you a sensation like . . . a life experience," Gregorio [an archive worker] recalled. "Like one of your friends had been there, that this was where they had been tortured, that maybe there were bodies buried there."[53]

Like the Atacama Desert, *la isla* and *el laberinto* were layered spaces, where the history of the past—buried bodies, mysterious holes—seeped into the present. Working there, archivists and activists (re)experienced "resurgent traumas, psychological burdens, and memories stirred by sorting through the archives."[54] Performing these "labors of memory" "brought these workers' dead back to life," achieving a kind of *aparición con vida* (appearance alive).[55] For example, based on evidence obtained in the archives, agents responsible for the disappearance of trade unionist Edgar Fernando García were prosecuted. Garcia's daughter, a lawyer, testified, "If my father is dead, he deserves to be buried like the beloved man that he was *and still is*, his name deserves dignity. He was not a sewer rat that can be killed with impunity; he was a human being."[56] Laboring in the archive excavated the past, insisting on the *life* of the dead and calling for accountability.

Just as "all of those cadavers had names," so too could the "*hombres desconocidos*" responsible for disappearances be identified.

Though painful, the memory work performed in the Guatemalan National Police archives promised to facilitate healing. As one archive worker commented, the archives were "a space where we all return to the past, and we all come to relive the pain or to awaken what's asleep inside each and every one of us, and to face the reality of what we lived."[57] Perhaps such awakenings overcame the separation between soul and body that Khosravi referred to as an "eternal nightmare."[58] Weld notes that according to Achille Mbembe, the work entailed in "following tracks, putting back together scraps and debris, and reassembling remains, is to be implicated in a ritual which results in the resuscitation of life, in bringing the dead back to life by reintegrating them in the cycle of time."[59] Such reintegration is a creative act; it returns to "the moment between forgetting and remembering the lived and the dreamed," moving out of the unintegrated and irresolute *estado de búsqueda* and into a "continuity of being."[60] As transitional objects, papers and other material remains can thus link multiple temporal planes.

Documentation

> My heart always beats faster at a book of blank pages than it does at any book filled with printing.
>
> Ruth Benedict, *An Anthropologist at Work*

Documents play key roles both as the objects of an *estado de búsqueda* and as bridges between past and future, events and evidence, subjectivity and objectification. Documents such as the blank pages that anthropologist Ruth Benedict longed to fill can seduce with their promise to record the present, reveal state secrets, bring an author (or ethnographer) into being, enable an encounter with the past, provide certainty, and transform social reality. Part of this seduction derives from the double vision that documents facilitate. On the one hand, documents provide a lens through which social reality can be assessed or viewed; they are evidence of the circumstances of their production, and they serve as external validation of preexisting social facts (death, birth, degree completion). On the other hand, documents can be considered artificial in that they create fictions that exist merely "on paper," produce the very facts that they allegedly authenticate, and hide truths that exceed that which can be documented.[61] Evidentiary yet fictitious, documents connect these disparate historical moments and different orders of being. For instance, as Beth Baker-Cristales points out, "Ethnographic writing is neither fiction nor science, but something inbetween."[62] Forging connections across this space "inbetween" is a creative process, a fictionalizing act, one in which "the world is created anew" as documents are redeployed in new circumstances or are returned to after the fact.[63]

Documents' ability to refer to that which lies outside their boundaries is another instance of abduction and lateral thinking. As we noted earlier, documents and that to which they refer appear to be the same thing but are also incommensurable. A birth certificate and a birth provide an example. The certificate appears to document the birth, yet in order for a birth and a certificate to be seen as equivalent, both must be abstracted into another order of knowledge, perhaps the legally cognizable.[64] Such abstraction is the process of abduction that, as we noted earlier, Bateson describes: a "double or multiple description of some object or event or sequence."[65] The creating of equivalence—that is, documents' ability to refer—is made possible by a creative leap across incommensurability. As filmmaker Gianfranco Rosi commented regarding the juxtapositions he deployed in *Fire at Sea*, "It's up to the viewer to interact and make his own connections. It's like a Giacometti statue, so thin, and *it's up to you to create the space that's missing*."[66] Here, Rosi's evocation of a Giacometti statue as a kind of transitional object that facilitates a leap across incommensurability underscores the ways that documentation can assume three-dimensional form. Whether as paper or as bone, cloth, or some other kind of representational material, the ways that documents are equivalent to yet incommensurable with their referents produces a kind of irresolution akin to what Hisham Matar, who grew up in exile, fantasized regarding New York, his place of birth: "I would imagine a new acquaintance asking me . . . that old tiresome question, 'Where are you from?' and I, unfazed and free of the usual agitation, would casually reply, 'New York.' In these fantasies, I saw myself taking pleasure from the fact that such a statement would be both true and false, like a magic trick."[67]

The irresolution between documents' ability to refer and their incommensurability with other orders of being gives documents a phantasmic quality associated with alive-deadness. Recall that Iser characterized the phantasm as "marked by the duality of simultaneously being present and not being taken for present; it is simultaneously something and not itself."[68] In the material that we have analyzed in this chapter, instances of documents being powerful yet absent abound. Matar sought evidence of his father's fate, the women in the Atacama Desert sought to learn what happened to their loved ones, the activists who rescued the Guatemalan National Police archives hoped to learn the truth about disappearances, Sophia Berzelius sought the truth about her birth mother's death and her own abandonment. In these cases, documents and other forms of evidence presumably existed, in some form, but could not always be accessed. In other cases, documents existed but should not have. For example, Khosravi had to travel with a

Greek passport under a name he could not even pronounce, and deportees received deportation orders despite their sense that they belonged in the United States. Individuals were also haunted by documents that should exist but did not: the papers that would allow migrants to have legal status, the valid travel documents that Khosravi wished he had, the visa that would allow a deportee (such as Greg, discussed in chapter 3) to return to the United States, perhaps a certificate for being born in *ninguna parte*. Perhaps the clearest example of the phantasmic quality of documents is the plans that architect Miguel drew up while imprisoned in Chacabuco. These were created and then destroyed, recorded only in Miguel's memory, where they served as documentation of a prison camp that was subsequently erased.

Through their phantasmic quality, documents act as if they are a form of evidence that brings past truths to bear on current realities. As we noted earlier, Iser draws on Vaihinger to describe the as if as "a kind of relay," perhaps a current that runs through and across different historical moments.[69] Documents can move through time, enabling one moment to be placed beside another. For example, if in 2018 one is looking at a record that the Guatemalan police produced in 1982, one is enabling these moments to partially merge, both in the past (in 1982) and in 2018. Thus, in 1982, the record of a dissident's disappearance is also future evidence in a prosecution, and in 2018, the same record is also the institutional memory of repression practiced in the 1980s. Documents preserve memory for the future. Matar's discovery of his father's published stories enabled him to encounter his father as a younger man, before Matar himself was born.

As they juxtapose and forge connections across disparate historical moments, documents also stand in for various sorts of subjects to which they are related. For example, documents in some ways reflect their authors. The records in the Guatemalan National Police archives reflect the perspective of the police, such that, as noted previously, former dissidents were "reencountering the war through the Other's eyes."[70] Likewise, the *expedientes*, or adoption files assembled during the thirty years of civil conflict in Guatemala, are populated by "a crowd" of subjects (mothers who give up their children, adoptive parents, temporary caregivers, witnesses, lawyers, and so forth) whose voices speak to the place of transnational adoption in the mechanisms of terror that were deployed during this period.[71] In addition, as we discussed in chapter 1, there is a doubling between ethnographers and fieldnotes, to the point that one ethnographer interviewed by Jean Jackson asserted, "I am a fieldnote."[72] Documents can also play a constitutive role in relation to the individuals about whom they are written. Adoption paperwork constitutes children as members of adoptive families, deportation orders can result in actual deportation, and being the subject of a police file in Guatemala in the 1980s could lead to torture and death. In one macabre case of such doubling, a disappeared person's fingers were attached to a fingerprint card, instead of just the finger-prints.[73] The term "paper cadavers" that Weld uses for the title of her book about the Guatemalan police archives evokes this duality. Even archive workers merged in some way with the documents they handled, literally breathing in the mold and dust of these decaying forms. As documents interacted with these different individuals—authors, referents, and archivists—they took on multiple identities and became a kind of connective tissue, not unlike the calcium that, in *Nostalgia for the Light,* connects the stars to the bone fragments found in the desert. In that they can reflect multiple subjectivities, the doubling between subject and docu-ment is often incomplete. Of the Guatemalan National Police archives, Weld ob-serves, "Survivors' memories did not necessarily square with the omissions, silences, and bureaucratic language of the documents," and María Elena, an ar-chive worker, told Weld, "I have found documents about my closest loved ones dead, their photos, very painful things. . . . But without necessarily finding any truths; sometimes you find nothing more than the stamp of repression upon their bodies."[74]

Bearing the stamp of repression—or of a particular set of experiences, as when ethnographers immerse themselves in a social milieu, using themselves as a research tool—can nonetheless create a vantage point from which to bear witness.[75] Patricio Guzmán, who directed *Nostalgia for the Light* and who was engaged in a lifelong project of using film to shed light on Pinochet's Chile, described himself as "a film-maker who was very marked by the ways of the dictator. It has remained with me forever. I cannot leave it behind."[76] Being "marked by the ways of the dictator" suggests a transference or imprint of sorts between Pinochet, Guzmán, and presumably other survivors. Noting that "Nobody knows what Pinochet did and nobody likes to talk about it," Guzmán sought to honor "those men and women who, in spite of Pinochet's secret police and death squads, fought for social justice."[77] He describes the process of looking through a camera as "not very different from looking through a telescope," and indeed, as Sandhu observes, "Guzmán himself could be said to be looking at Chile through a telescope," a project that began with an earlier film, *The Battle of Chile,* in which documentary was used "as a tool for countering state lies, showcasing subaltern testimonies and fashioning brave new aesthetics."[78] By directing the gaze of his telescope on the truths that the dictatorship sought to erase and with which Chilean society may not have fully grappled, Guzmán documents the existent nonrealities that lie back of lives and worlds.[79]

BEYOND "SPOOKY ACTION AT A DISTANCE"

An Ethnography of the Future

> **Which is farther from us, farther out of reach, more silent—the dead, or the unborn? Those whose bones lie under the thistles and the dirt and the tombstones of the Past, or those who slip weightless among molecules, dwelling where a century passes in a day, among the fair folk, under the great, bell-curved Hill of Possibility?**
>
> Ursula K. Le Guin, *Always Coming Home*

Science fiction writer and quasi-anthropologist Ursula K. Le Guin's novel *Always Coming Home* is an ethnography of a future society, the Kesh, who "might be going to have lived a long, long time from now in Northern California."[1] This work reassembles the Kesh through fragments that make up something of a whole but that, due to the impossibility of fully representing nontextual realities in written form, can never be complete. The narrative portion of the book features the first-person life story of a woman called Stone Telling, divided into three parts, interspersed with folktales, sketches, poetry, histories, and ethnographic observations collected by an archivist or editor. This material is followed by a section titled "The Back of the Book," which resembles a classic ethnography, with kinship charts, descriptions of rituals, a glossary, maps, songs, and information about material culture. To write this book, Le Guin says that she had to translate from "a language that doesn't yet exist."[2] Pointing out that no translation can replicate the original, she suggests that "the mere absence of a text to translate doesn't make all that much difference. What was and what may be lie, like children whose faces we cannot see, in the arms of silence. All we ever have is here, now."[3]

Deeply nostalgic for a potential culture that has not yet come into being, Le Guin's "archaeology of the future" plays with time, space, and voice, mingling past and future, the explicit and the unstated, observer and those who produce their own accounts, culture and individual, and the "home" to which people return and from which they cannot be fully severed.[4] The book's protagonist, Stone Telling, who had multiple names throughout her lifetime, is a "half-House" or "half a person," the daughter of a Blue Clay mother and a Condor father.[5] Like the refugees, migrants, adoptees, exiles, and relatives of the disappeared whose lives we have recounted here, Stone Telling lives between worlds, belonging to yet an outsider in both Sinshan, where her mother lived, and the City of the Condor, where her father originated. This experience gave her binocular vision: "All that grieved me—that I was half one thing and half another and nothing wholly—was the sorrow of my childhood, but the strength and use of my life after I grew up."[6] Unlike her parents, who "could see with one eye only," Stone Telling saw "with one eye" and "with the other eye."[7] Binocular vision gave her a kind of wisdom: "We have to learn what we can, but remain mindful that our knowledge not close the circle, closing out the void, so that we forget that what we do not know remains boundless, without limit or bottom, and that what we know may have to share the quality of being known with what denies it. What is seen with one eye has no depth."[8]

In addition to learning to see with both eyes, Stone Telling found that departing Sinshan to live among the Condor people revealed that she was almost physically connected to the places she called home: "I began to feel the Valley behind me like a body, my own body. My feet were the sea-channels of the River, the organs and passages of my body were the places and streams and my bones the rocks and my head was the Mountain. That was all my body, and I here lying down was a breath-soul, going farther away from its body every day. A long very thin string connected that body and that soul, a string of pain."[9] Her words here are reminiscent of the deep connection to the United States that Greg had following deportation to El Salvador (see chapter 3); that Amanda, a Swedish adoptee, felt for Ethiopia as "the reality I live in" after meeting her birth parents there (see chapter 1); and that exile Shahram Khosravi experienced when images from his past life in Iran suddenly erupted during his daily life in Sweden (see chapter 4). Indeed, Stone Telling, Greg, Amanda, and Shahram Khosravi all experienced something of an *estado de búsqueda*, living in multiple spaces at the same time.

Though it is a fictional account, the temporal and spatial dimensions of Le Guin's archaeology of the future—and also of the *estado de búsqueda*, the elsewhere that pulls on the known—in some ways resonate with emerging understandings of time, space, and possibility within quantum physics, understandings that Albert Einstein disparagingly termed "spooky action at a distance."[10] According to quantum theory, what may appear to be separate phenomena may, if they share an origin, actually be connected even if they are quite distant from each other: "When particles originate under certain conditions, quantum theory predicts that a measurement of one particle will correlate with the state of another particle even if the distance between the particles is millions of light-years."[11] As a result, an impact on one of the particles affects both of them, a principle known as "quantum entanglement."[12] The principle of entanglement suggests that what appear to be unrelated entities are in fact part of an indiscernible whole. Nadeau and Kafatos explain:

> This reality . . . manifests as an indivisible or undivided whole whose existence is "inferred" where there is an interaction with an observer, or with instruments of observation. . . . An indivisible whole contains, by definition, no separate parts and . . . a phenomenon can be assumed to be "real" only when it is an "observed" phenomenon. . . . [So] the indivisible whole whose existence is inferred . . . cannot in principle be itself the subject of scientific investigation. . . . Science can claim knowledge of physical reality only when the predictions of a physical theory are validated by experiment.[13]

Recent exchanges among quantum theorists have extended the interpretation of quantum mechanics to include a cosmological perspective. These discussions have focused on how to conceptualize an indiscernible whole (like the universe, for example) when each observer is restricted to his or her own "causal patch" or "cosmic horizon."[14] Some quantum theorists have conjectured about a "multiverse" rather than a universe, but the fundamental question of "how to piece together our splintered stories into some single arena we call the universe"— or even an array of multiverses—remains unresolved.[15] Conjectures about a multiverse open up the possibility that any such undivided whole can only be an illusion—"a papier-mâché construction of our imagination in between the solid iron pillars of our observations."[16]

Perhaps most promising in terms of providing a template for our ethnographic project on how impossible realities can be mapped or documented is the posited relationship between two seemingly different model universes, theorized as "holographic equivalence" by physicist Juan Maldacena in 1997.[17] One is a cosmos similar to our own that is four-dimensional, obeys Einstein's equations of gravity, and is known as "the bulk"; the other (known as "the boundary") has one dimension fewer and provides a gravity-free space onto which the more complex (gravity-dominated) relations that rule in the bulk can be mapped, giving physicists a new way to think about gravity.[18] What became known as "Maldacena's duality" provided physicists "with a way to think about quantum gravity in the bulk without thinking about gravity at all; they just had to look at the equivalent quantum state on the boundary."[19] The boundary-bulk correspondence is completely nonlocal in that the information that corresponds to a small region of the bulk is spread over a vast region of the boundary in which quantum particles are entangled. As a result, the boundary generates "a ghostly quantum phenomenon of entanglement" that in turn appears as a "geometric glue" in the bulk region that may be, according to recent conjecture, "what knits space-time into a smooth whole."[20]

Interestingly, there seems to be a clear parallel between the way that acts of observation or measurement in quantum physics make it possible to infer the existence of a ghostly but indivisible whole, and the role of ethnographers who infer "culture" through its manifestations in ritual, language, exchange, and other phenomena. Moreover, the principle of nonlocality seemingly applies to time as well as space. Nadeau and Kafatos write that the results of quantum mechanical experiments "not only show that the observer and the observed system cannot be separate and distinct in space. They also reveal that this distinction does not exist in time. It is as if we caused something to happen 'after' it has already occurred. . . . The past is inexorably mixed with the present and even the phenomenon of time is tied to specific experimental choices."[21] Taking these lessons from quantum theory into account, it is perhaps not surprising that Le Guin could produce an ethnography of a possible future society, or that Stone Telling found herself inextricably interconnected to the Valley that she was leaving behind.

The ways that "spooky" quantum physics coexists with the more commonsense understandings of time, space, movement, and location that are part of classical physics in some ways parallels the impossible realities that we have explored in this book. Classical physics presumes that objects exist in particular locations, that time is linear, that space can be mapped, that theory corresponds to the physical world, and that scientific observations exist outside the phenomena they measure. These presumptions work well most of the time, allowing engineers and scientists to rely on classical physics when designing bridges and computers and when planning space travel. Quantum theory, however, provides a more fundamental description of physical phenomena. Most of the time, the differences between quantum and classical calculations and predictions are so minute that they are insignificant, enabling scientists to act as if classical theory works. At extremes of scale, however, such as the microscale and situations with extreme mass concentrations, classical theory breaks down. Likewise, it is possible to act as if the world works according to legal conventions: that people belong to the society where they are born, that biological relationships are the basis for kinship, that there are orderly ways to cross national borders, that people do not simply disappear, and that it is impossible to be alive and dead at the same time. Yet in the nowhere occupied by those who are in an *estado de búsqueda*, these conventions break down and, as Stone Telling noted, "what we know may have to share the quality of being known with what denies it."

Relationality

> Shevek's "revelation . . . the way clear, the way home, the light" (9:280) is not the elimination of the distinction between Sequency and Simultaneity, but the discovery of a relationship.
>
> Everett L. Hamner, "The Gap in the Wall: Partnership, Physics and Politics,"
> writing about Ursula K. Le Guin's *The Dispossessed*

In this book, we have explored the *as if* as a relationship between interconnected yet seemingly incompatible phenomena: law and the illicit, adoptive and biological kinship, the world in which people are compelled to cross borders and the world in which nations govern movement, the state as a perpetrator of human rights abuses and the state as guarantor of national security, alive-deadness and disappearance, trace and erasure, the quality of being known and what denies being known. It is difficult to determine which of these is real and which is counterfeit. For example, it is tempting to see adoptive kinship as an imitation of biological relationships: adopted relatives act (and are meant to be regarded) as if they are biological kin. Indeed, this version of adoption has provided a rationale for inserting a clean break between adoptees and birth mothers, so that the naturalness of the newly constituted adoptive family will not be disrupted by the intrusion of the legally dissolved biological family. Yet because all children are potentially alienable if their biological parents abandon them or place them for adoption, or if they are involuntarily removed from their families, biological relationships also have a (usually unacknowledged and perhaps unrealized) as-if dimension: these relationships could have been otherwise. This "otherwise" is powerfully predetermined by *law* (for example, in the form of a birth certificate that establishes parental ties) but may be unsettled when figure and ground change place—when, for example, adopted children are "adopted" back into their birth family or when children who were adopted from abroad by US parents but who were never naturalized learn that they can be deported. French anthropologist and adoptee Elise Prébin compares such unsettling circumstances to "the common metaphor that describes anthropologists as being adopted by their informants." As Prébin explains: "My relationship with my birth family [in Korea] has . . . led me to rethink and reevaluate the ties I built with my adoptive family. Whereas in the past I could only compare my adoptive relationships to biological relationships, I can now put them in relief to the relationships I have created with my birth relatives after adoption and meeting. . . . So in the end, my experience over time challenged the idea that biological birth produces noncontingent or necessary ties and that adoption produces contingent or free ones."[22]

As we noted in chapter 1, adoption signals the naturalness of biological kinship in that it positions adopted child and adoptive parents in relation to an imagined (but officially sanctioned) biological "real" of which they are only counterfeit renditions. In this sense, the felt need to return is placed at the core of an adoptive relationship, even as an adoption decree makes such a movement impossible by canceling a preexisting (biological, natural) state. But if this state is by definition one that preexists law, how can it be canceled by law? Recall the case of Greg (see chapter 3), whose adoptive parents in the United States did not understand that they had to apply for Greg's naturalization but whose deportation to El Salvador "returned" him to a (biological) state that no longer existed—in effect, *ninguna parte*—because it had been canceled by law. As these examples suggest, adoptive and biological kinship exist in relation to each other and, in a sense, bring each other into being, even as conventional accounts of kinship depict biology as real and adoption as a fiction. Their interrelationship is therefore somewhat like the solution that the physicist Shevek, a character in Le Guin's 1974 novel, *The Dispossessed*, devises to what is known as Zeno's paradox: "As Shevek realizes, if he throws a rock at a tree, the rock must at some point be halfway between him and the tree, and then at some point halfway between *that* point and the tree, and so on into infinity. Theoretically, the rock should never reach the tree. Of course it does."[23] To account for both sequency ("the succession of instants") and simultaneity (according to which "rock-throwing and tree-hitting constitute a single action"), Shevek places these in relationship, such that "the 'arrow' of time and the 'circle' of time together create an arrow that spirals forward."[24] While the discovery of this relationship is a science fiction device, attention to this potential relationship evokes quantum theory's view of reality as an indivisible whole.[25]

The movement between reality and the unreal, like that between adoption and biology or perhaps sequence and simultaneity, can be described as a current, the sort of current that we described in chapter 1. This current passes through and connects conjoined realities (worlds, universes, conscious and unconscious states, conditions such as "adopted" or "biological" relationships), whose boundaries cannot be seen because when one reality is visible, the other is invisible. So, to continue to tease out the example of adoption and biology, both biological and adoptive kinship are equally natural and unnatural, as explained earlier, yet the unnaturalness of biology and the naturalness of adoption are invisible within conventional accounts of kinship (though they are *not* invisible to anthropologists—and may also become visible when adoptees "return" to what was imagined as a "biological" ground, as was the case in the preceding examples).[26] Apprehending these invisible dimensions requires the depth of vision that Gregory Bateson termed "binocular" or "double description," so as to see biology and adoption from two vantage points: from the perspective afforded by knowledge of children's alienability (which reveals kinship to be a legal relationship) and from the understanding that adoption is simultaneously a destination and an origin (which reveals biology to be irrelevant to the family brought into being through adoption). The relationship between kinship as sequence (as in multiple generations or linkages between genetic material) and kinship as simultaneous (as bringing a singular constellation of relationships into being) gives rise to temporal arrows spiraling in multiple directions. These movements between the impossible and the necessary, between truth and that which cannot be, produce an energy that fuels creative inventions. Recall, for example, Janice's discussion (in chapter 3) of the "missing middle" and the limitations of teachers' and other adults' depictions of Black girls' lives. Janice advocates "surviving by holding onto our truth. The truth you don't see in TV or in the papers."[27] In a similar way, Araceli Muñoz, a temporary protected status recipient who was born in El Salvador but grew up in Los Angeles, described her experience of home as multifaceted, defined not so much by the legal technicalities of birthplace but rather by "where you grew up, where you spend most of your childhood, where . . . you learned what you know," a truth of belonging that is excluded from her official definition as a "temporary" resident of the United States (see chapter 2).

In this book, we have drawn on work by object relations psychologist D. W. Winnicott and anthropologist Gregory Bateson, among others, as these theorists provide ways of thinking about the form of creativity in which existent nonrealities make themselves felt through a "logic of similarities."[28] In a similar way, Elise Prébin's dissertation project as an anthropologist involved analyzing a popular morning talk show on Korean TV in which highly scripted reunions of parents and children who had been separated for years (including separations due to transnational adoption) were aired.[29] This juxtaposition of different kinds of separation and the reunions that ensued on the TV show became a kind of script for Prébin's own discovery of the continuity between kinship as relatedness in the context of her adoption by French parents and the relatedness she was experiencing in her reunion with her birth mother and relatives of her birth father in Seoul. As Prébin explained, "The South Korean televised meetings create a moment that helps to define a type of transatlantic relatedness in historically and culturally acceptable terms. Problematic because they are past and yet present, lingering and yet severed, inalienable and yet unacceptable, blood ties are turned into a middle-ground alternative, a relatedness that combines and accepts a plurality of belongings and fluidity of identities."[30]

Prébin's experience illuminates how the current or movement between the official reality of biological kinship and the as-if reality of adoption are mutually constitutive of each other, in a complex process of recognition and reversal in which the figure of the adoptee travels home in both directions.[31] The as-if status of adoption propels both the cancellation of so-called blood ties and the pull to a "back" that marks these ties as real, instantiating both the difference between adoptive and biological ties and recognition of adoption as a "support bridge over the unfathomable breaks in continuity, which are felt as a threat."[32]

Like adoption, other phenomena that are connected in an as-if relationship bring each other into being and create dual vantage points. For example, national immigration systems establish an allegedly orderly system according to which individuals are citizens of different countries and can travel to other territories only if they possess authorization to do so. Yet this system actually creates so-called illegal immigration, even though authorities act as if unauthorized movement were not a product of their own interventions. As legal scholar Catherine Dauvergne concludes, "The current 'crackdown' on extralegal migration cannot help but increase it."[33] In a sense, immigration officials gain authority through unauthorized immigrants' efforts to evade them, even as authorities' efforts to police borders and restrict access to status simultaneously give rise to the illicit world of smugglers, forged documents, and hidden compartments, as suggested in our discussion of the emergence and transformation of *coyoterismo* in chapter 2.[34] In this mutual imbrication, the border between licit and illicit movement can dissolve, as when undocumented immigrants perceive the fees that they have to submit along with applications for legal status as analogous to the payments they must make to smugglers, or when Congress authorizes granting lawful permanent residency to anyone who invests at least $1 million in the US economy.[35] At the same time, when viewed externally, the mutuality of the gaze between law enforcement and unauthorized movement creates a border, suggesting that each is a different phenomenon, just as in physics, when the act of measurement fixes the locations of nonlocalized particles.

The temporality of as-if relationships is also complex, in ways that evoke Shevek's solution to Zeno's paradox. On the one hand, it appears that these relationships are established sequentially: first biology, then adoption; first nation-states, then unauthorized immigration; first home, then exile; first life, then death; first trace, then erasure. On the other hand, biological kinship depends on a contrast with kinship by law; the ability to regulate international movement is a hallmark of sovereignty; those who live in exile may simultaneously experience eruptions of images of home; the disappeared exist in an alive-dead state; and the plans of a clandestine prison can be reconstructed after the fact.[36] To once again draw from object relations theory, if a parent's gaze establishes a baby's sense of self, and if a baby becomes a person through a parent seeing the person in the baby, then the future (the parent's recognition of the baby) can precede the present (the baby existing), and the past (the version of the baby that compelled the parent's recognition) occurs after the present (the baby taking form upon being recognized by the parent). This quote from Nadeau and Kafatos is once again apt: "It is as if we caused something to happen 'after' it has already occurred. . . . The past is inexorably mixed with the present and even the phenomenon of time is tied to specific experimental choices."[37] In addition to occurring sequentially, therefore, phenomena that are placed in an as-if relationship exist beside each other, as continuity between phenomena becomes contiguity between them, giving rise to the possibility of new arrangements—perhaps justice for victims of disappearances, a world in which multiple origins can be acknowledged, and accountability for the policies and practices that compel unauthorized movement in the first place.

We have advocated being open to the as if in exploring the "existent 'nonrealit[ies]'" that are created when "something" (fiction?) is "suddenly divided off from something else which—even if not 'real'—is nevertheless there."[38] This location is difficult to sustain because the realities that it conjoins are incompatible. *Ninguna parte*—the "nowhere" occupied by those who are adopted, who live in exile, who are in an *estado de búsqueda*, or who migrate—is often part of the same world occupied by everyone else and can be located in such places as Germany, Chile, Korea, Sweden, the United States, and El Salvador. Individuals are placed in such a "nonlocation" through practices of exclusion that forbid them to fully be or that render their existence indeterminate, making them as if. Yet figure and ground can shift. The work of filmmakers, artists, activists, ethnographers, searchers, and others can reframe social reality, opening up a potential space, "an intermediate area of *experiencing* to which inner reality and external life both contribute" and where boundaries can be traversed.[39] A refrain chanted at a recent immigrant rights march, which was also a slogan at the 1999 World Trade Organization protests in Seattle, comes to mind: "Otro mundo es posible, no tenemos que vivir así." (Another world is possible, we don't have to live like this.)[40]

Accessing this other world requires moving against the current in ways that threaten the very classifications on which modernity is based: nature–culture, human–nonhuman, belonging–nonbelonging, inside–outside. The as if is a way of managing these dichotomies: it maintains the illusion of distinct forms with clear boundaries, even as the forms and the boundaries that seem to contain them are constantly being transgressed by the so-called unauthorized, adopted, transgender, criminal, and subversive. These transgressions approximate the real in ways that imply the alienability of real belongings and make visible the dynamic involved in producing the modern through its counterfeit forms. Yet the as if is also emotionally fraught, because approximating but not being able to reach a real (or what is officially recognized as such) can be devastating. The concept of "as if" therefore captures a kind of longing for a real (pure) form that is always just out of reach and that is somehow emblematic of the modern, even as adoptive identities, the unauthorized, and in some sense the ethnographer embody the tension between this real and that which is cut off from it.[41]

Law, Fiction, and Ethnography

> The "total reality" of a quantum system is wave and particle. . . . In addition to representing profound oppositions that preclude one another in a given situation, both constructs are necessary to achieve a complete understanding of the entire situation. In other words, it is both logically disparate constructs that describe the total reality even though only one can be applied in any given instance.
>
> Robert Nadeau and Menas Kafatos, *The Non-local Universe*

The sort of binocular vision that we have analyzed in this book and that Le Guin's character Stone Telling describes makes it possible to discern "logically disparate constructs that describe the total reality," including the total reality made up by law and the worlds that law prohibits. For example, law prohibits baby selling, unauthorized border crossings, the smuggling of individuals, and political disorder. At the same time, these practices are defined by and therefore could not exist without law. As a result, there is a sort of self-referentiality in the relationship between law and illegality such that illegality is the constitutive outside of law and also internal to it.[42] Adoptees, deportees, immigrants, exiles, prisoners, and political dissidents are dislocated to the elsewhere that law prohibits: the underground, the shadows, clandestinity, the netherworld. These non-spaces simultaneously cannot be—as they are prohibited—but also must be, in that without them, law would know no boundaries and have nothing to govern. As we conveyed through Tucker Nichols's Venn diagram in chapter 1, impossible realities exist at the intersection of what must be yet cannot be real. These existent nonrealities pull on law, challenging its truths in ways that are destabilizing. Awareness of what might be described as the total reality consisting of law and illegality potentially denaturalizes the systems that make immigrants, adoptees, exiles, refugees, and dissidents "impossible subjects" who cannot yet must exist.[43]

Gregory Bateson's account of the relationship between "strict" and "loose" thinking—discussed in chapter 3—provides a way to explore what lies outside law's boundaries. Bateson points out that there is something of a cycle between the structure provided by established "concepts, postulates, and premises" and the creativity that comes from an "orgy of loose thinking" in which these foundations are questioned. Bateson recommends "train[ing] them [scholars, scientists] to tie knots in their handkerchiefs whenever they leave some matter unformulated—to be willing to leave the matter so for years, but still leave a warning sign in the very terminology they use, such that these terms will forever stand, not as fences hiding the unknown from future investigators, but rather as signposts which read: 'UNEXPLORED BEYOND THIS POINT.'"[44] Adoptees, noncitizens, exiles, and others who populate *ninguna parte* demarcate such unknown and uncertain domains, bringing forward earlier moments in time while also gesturing toward alternative presents and futures. The Swedish poet Tomas Tranströmer's poem "Answers to Letters" conveys the temporal complexity of such movements: "Sometimes an abyss opens between Tuesday and Wednesday but twenty-six years may be passed in a moment. Time is not a straight line, it's more of a labyrinth, and if you press close to the wall at the right place you can hear the hurrying steps and the voices, you can hear yourself walking past there on the other side."[45] Tranströmer's words are reminiscent of Matar's description of imagining that he would encounter an earlier version of himself in Benghazi, or Guatemalan archive workers' awareness that friends and compatriots could have been tortured in the very spaces that they were excavating. Thus, law's attempts to demarcate past and present through clean breaks, such as those provided by adoption or naturalization, also place seemingly different moments side by side. Sequence, as Shevek noted, cannot be divorced from simultaneity.

Yet acting as if legality and illegality or sequence and simultaneity can be clearly differentiated allows the world to assume its current form. Fiction is therefore a kind of device, current, or relay that connects that which must be yet cannot be real. For example, undocumented students who are advocating for a means to legalize their presence in the United States *must* be "American", in that they grew up in the United States and in many cases know no other country, but also (according to some) *cannot* be "American", because they lack legal status. They are positioned as simultaneously akin to yet fundamentally different from other "Americans" and therefore occupy an impossible subject position in an existent nonreality. The citizen–alien distinctions that complicate their lives are considered real, at least in a legal sense, but also derive from nationalist fantasies about citizens' superiority, intrinsic belonging, and the racialized differences that supposedly mark citizens' distance from "noncitizens." A similar argument is put forward by ethnographer Aimee Cox, who re-positions the Black girls at the center of her analysis as "shapeshifters," exploring their insistence on shifting the terms through which social service institutions seek to shape young Black women into respectable citizens.[46] In a related move, legal theorist Patricia Williams sought to shift the conventions of legal writing by making clear the gaps such conventions required of her, in this way forcing her readers to participate in making (officially) impossible meanings real.[47] In fact, if the reality narrated in all these outsider accounts is privileged, then the structures that situated them outside the legal and political order come to seem fantastical. Yet the differences imagined in nationalist fantasies are not tangible, in that, as Bateson points out, differences only become apparent in a relationship involving comparison, the "differences that make a difference."[48] To illustrate this idea, Bateson uses the example of chalk on a board. When people look at the mark left by the chalk, they may see a white spot, but where is the spot? It is neither in the chalk nor in the board but rather in the difference between them.[49]

Though it may be intangible, fiction is not false and can in fact be quite powerful. Take the example of gravity. One of the fundamental laws of physics, as articulated by Isaac Newton, is that a particle attracts every other particle with a force that is inversely proportional to the square of the distance between their centers, "the inverse square law."[50] Yet, as previously discussed, quantum physics has rethought this description of gravity to instead conclude that gravity is "a pure quantum effect" that arises when interactions between entangled particles on the boundary of a specific model of the universe result in increasing complexity.[51] Complexity, according to Stanford University physicist Leonard Susskind, "behaves much like a gravitational field" because of "the way that interactions between the boundary particles cause an explosive growth in the complexity of their collective quantum state."[52] For Susskind, this principle became a saying: "Things fall because there is a tendency toward complexity."[53] Instead of being a force that attracts objects, gravity is an effect of complexity. As physics and cosmology writer Amanda Gefter observes, this means that the "deepest thing we know about gravity" is that "it emerges as a holographic projection. That it's an illusion. That it's not real."[54]

Likewise, many of the forces that determine whether people are deemed to belong or to be outsiders have a fictive quality. Biology appears to be a force that determines kinship but in fact may be an effect of presuming that particular relationships exist. Law appears to be a force that differentiates citizens from noncitizens, but citizenship and alienage are themselves legal fictions that overlay persons, becoming visible when individuals are deemed to not belong. National security would seem to mandate that potential threats be investigated, but the creation of police files about particular Guatemalan dissidents was used as justification for their assassination or disappearance, even if they were nonviolent. Law, biology, and national security therefore have a phantasmic quality: "The phantasm is marked by the duality of simultaneously being present and not being taken for present; it is simultaneously something and not itself. *It becomes the medium for the appearance of what is not.*"[55] Law, biology, and national security doctrine thus make possible the appearance of subjects who, impossibly, embody these contradictions: *alien* citizens, *adopted* kin, and *Guatemalan* dissidents.

A key role of ethnography, then, is to document such appearances. To do so, ethnographers follow transitional objects and beings, including archives like the

Guatemalan one, detritus and fragments like those found in the Atacama Desert, records like those in the Ethiopian orphanage, exilic states of being like those of Hisham Matar and Khosravi, or unauthorized immigrants who are simultaneously invisible and in the center of Los Angeles. Such journeys transcend the distinction between sequence and simultaneity. Thus, an ethnographer such as Kristen Weld, who wrote about the Guatemalan police archives, conducted fieldwork at particular moments, but also through her fieldwork was brought into the realities that the archives and the archive workers conveyed, and these realities transcended the temporal limits of her fieldwork. Recall Weld's observation that "reencountering the war through the Other's eyes blurred comfortable distinctions between present and past, memory and history. In Esperanza's [her interlocutor's] words, the archives were 'a space where we all return to the past, and we all come to relive the pain or to awaken what's asleep inside each and every one of us, and to face the reality of what we lived.' . . . They continually relived past experiences while performing contemporary memory labor."[56] Weld herself returned to the past through her fieldwork, a past that she had not directly experienced, even as she became part of efforts to envision a more just future in Guatemala, one in which perpetrators of abuse would be brought to justice and in which the disappeared would appear alive "by reintegrating them in the cycle of time" and being recognized as full human beings.[57]

By bringing separate moments together, ethnography has the potential to create something new: an ethnographic account that must be real because it is based on observations, but that also cannot be real because it reflects the perspective of the ethnographer. Interestingly, physicists too have concluded that observers have the creative potential to bring reality into being. If, as Schrödinger's thought experiment involving a cat, a box, and a photon suggests (see chapter 3), a photon potentially exists in multiple states at the same time and only resolves into a single state through the measurement taken by an observer, then in the end, *the* observer (a singular observer) makes the universe.[58] Or, to put it differently, the "unbounded homogeneity" of "nothing" is disrupted by the presence of an observer, who makes the infinite finite in the sense that the observer's frame of reference is limited by a particular horizon.[59] In the case of ethnographers, this particular horizon is provided by the field, which focuses and delimits an ethnographer's gaze even as the field is itself brought into being through the presence of the ethnographer. Of course, the boundaries around ethnographic fields are fluid, a fact that again parallels physicists' conclusions about their own scientific practices. Wheeler argued that "Elementary phenomena are impossible without the distinction between observing equipment and observed system . . . but the line of distinction can run like a maze, so convoluted that what appears from one standpoint to be on one side and to be identified as observing apparatus, from another point of view has to be looked at as observed system. . . . Aren't we mistaken in making this separation between 'the universe' and 'life and mind'?"[60]

Obviating such distinctions can occur through immersion in the field, which is also a kind of nonlocality or existent nonreality. An ethnographic field is entangled, in the quantum physics sense, in that actions taken there reverberate outside the field, and vice versa, as the ethnographer moves between them. If an ethnographer were participating in Schrödinger's thought experiment, then the ethnographer would likely not only be taking the measurement that determined the photon's location but also be in the box, with the cat, in the alive-dead state that characterizes those in an *estado de búsqueda*. Hence, the emotional pulls that affect immigrants, exiles, dissidents, refugees, and adoptees affect ethnographers as well, who of course can themselves be immigrants, exiles, dissidents, refugees, and adoptees.

Boundaries and Ladders

> Anti–de Sitter space is a pretty special space. . . . It's like putting gravity in a box. But the problem that many of us keep coming back to is that we don't live in a box. There are no walls to our universe. So that's the question that needs to be answered.
>
> Amanda Gefter, *Trespassing on Einstein's Lawn*, quoting the physicist Joe Polchinski, of UC Santa Barbara

In order to explore the nature of the universe, physicists have developed the notion of anti–de Sitter (AdS) space, which "describes a cosmos that is like our own Universe in the sense that everything in it, including black holes, is governed by gravity. Unlike our Universe, however, it has a boundary—a domain where there is no gravity, just elementary particles and fields governed by quantum physics. Despite this difference, studying physics in AdS has led to many insights, because every object and process inside the space can be mathematically mapped to an equivalent object or process on its boundary."[61] The boundary around anti–de Sitter space is useful, in that it enables particular kinds of calculations, but anti–de Sitter space's utility stems from its relationship to what lies on the other side of the boundary, namely the universe as we know it. Gefter explains, "Calculations that are complicated in one domain often turn out to be simple in the other. And after the calculations are complete, the insights gained in AdS can generally be translated back into our own Universe."[62]

What is on the other side of the boundaries established by law? A recent series of articles written by birth mothers and critical adoption scholars asserts that the clean break established by law is anything but clean. Janet Mason Ellerby found that even when birth mothers were reunited with their adult children, "our happy ending dissolved. We still longed for the past. The deed could not be reversed. The baby could not be restored. The longing could not be assuaged."[63] Eric Walker pointed out that "throughout adoption writing, what is always at stake is the presence of absence."[64] The emotional anguish associated with adoption pulls at all involved, in ways that, to paraphrase Laura Briggs, make hypervisible the contradictions that pervade "public" and "private" as "fictions of liberal political theory."[65]

We conclude therefore with an image that transcends boundaries, namely a ladder of light that, in November 2017, the artists Jill Marie Holslin and Andrew Sturm and the activist Larry Pierce of San Diego Overpass Light Brigade projected onto a prototype for the border wall that Donald Trump wanted to build.[66] Holslin explained to a journalist, "The ladder is this simple, simple thing—you can buy a ladder for $50 and you can climb over a wall that they spent $500,000 to build. . . . It's this simple technology that defeats every effort of the government to create this massive image of impermeability and absolute power."[67]

FIGURE 5.1. Jill Marie Holslin, visual artist, *Escalera*, from the series *Testing Trump's Wall*, 2017. Holslin was the lead artist on the series and the public art project. Courtesy of Testing Trump's Wall.

In this case, the ladder itself may be a fiction, but the light is not. Like the light that fascinated astronomers in the Atacama Desert, we hope that our book has provided a ladder out of the boxes that limit thinking, enabling us, like the cat in Schrodinger's thought experiment and Ursula K. Le Guin's short story, to go elsewhere.

Notes

PROLOGUE

1. Yngvesson 2005, 30; see also Nelsen 2021.

2. In presenting this history of our collaboration, we explicate what lies behind our work. The title of this prologue comes from Margaret Mead's introduction to the collected papers of Ruth Benedict (1959, xv–xvi). The full passage reads, "In any generation there may be a group of people who find meaning in just these unrecorded parts of life, who can read a book the better for knowing what the author meant to write while writing something else, or who even catch a glimpse of excitement from a first edition if they know also how the writer felt on the day those crisp fresh pages first met his eye. Particularly today there is great interest throughout the world in 'becoming' rather than in completed form, in the latent image and in the counterpoint between almost forgotten words and new, unimagined meanings. And so it seems a possible enterprise to try to set down such a piece of oral history as lies back of the work of Ruth Benedict, who came, unexpectedly, into a young science and shaped her thought into a book which for a generation has stood as a bridge between those who cherish the uniqueness of individual achievement and those who labor to order the regularities in all human achievement."

3. Here we are paraphrasing Heller's (2021, 1) essay about Joan Didion, who wrote about "what holds society together, or tears it apart."

4. The anthropologist Leo Chavez (2013), for example, writes about the fear that Latinx immigrants threaten to "take over" the United States, and news stories sometimes recount experiences of individuals who *thought* they were US citizens, only to discover that in fact they were born outside the country and were never naturalized (see, for example, Hennessy-Fiske 2019). The Abuelas de Plaza de Mayo have spent decades trying to recover grandchildren who were presumably adopted into other families when these children's parents were disappeared during military rule in Argentina. This scenario is dramatized in the film *La historia oficial* (The Official Story).

5. See Cox 2015 for a discussion of the importance of treating research participants' accounts as sources of theory; and see Schindele 2022 for an example of the transformation of a research participant's account into a subsequent theoretical account that is published by the participant.

6. See Heller 2021, 5.

7. Einstein used this phrase in a letter to Max Born in 1947 (see Born 2005, 155) in the context of an exchange with Born about the failure of quantum mechanics to provide a complete description of physical reality. As he wrote to Born, "I cannot seriously believe in [the statistical approach which Born advanced] . . . because the theory cannot be reconciled with the idea that physics should represent a reality in time and space, free from spooky action at a distance. . . . But I am quite convinced that someone will eventually come up with a theory whose objects, connected by laws, are not probabilities but considered facts, as used to be taken for granted until quite recently." See also Einstein, Podolsky, and Rosen 1935, which is "often credited with bringing the notion of entangled quantum states and action at a distance to the attention of the physics community" (Boughn 2018, 2), although as Boughn notes, "The conclusion of EPR was not that quantum mechanics

was nonlocal nor that objective reality did not exist but rather that quantum mechanics 'does not provide a complete description of the physical reality.'" We take up the issue of quantum entanglement in more detail in chapters 1 and 5.

1. COUNTERFEITING REALITY

1. In suggesting that ethnographers foreground counterfeited forms of reality as a way of making visible the limitations of conventional accounts of who does or does not belong in a family or polity, we are not suggesting that truth is relative, nor are we condoning corrupt governments' efforts to skew election outcomes or create their own versions of truth. Rather, we highlight the ways that inequality is reconstrued as wrongdoing or fraud on the part of marginalized peoples who are treated as suspect, and we explore the contingency of an official "real" on the as ifs or counterfeits that ground it—the as-if-begotten child that makes a family complete, the unauthorized worker whose labor is essential to the functioning of everyday life. Our goal is to highlight the concept of form in the construction of reality and to illuminate its shadow other, the ground without which reality cannot be seen (see especially the "Currents" section with which we conclude this chapter, and our discussion of Gregory Bateson's concept of binocular vision in chapter 2).

2. Ms. L. v. US Immigration and Customs Enforcement, 310 F. Supp. 3d 1133, 1137 (S.D. Cal. 2018).

3. See United States District Court, Southern District of California 2018.

4. Congressional Research Service 2021.

5. López 2021.

6. Gomberg-Muñoz 2016.

7. See Mitchell and Coutin 2019. One of us—Susan—observed an appointment between Helena, who was a US citizen, and a paralegal who was helping her petition for her sister, who was in El Salvador. To prove they were sisters, Helena and her sister needed to provide their birth certificates, showing that they had the same parents. Unfortunately, their father's name was not on the certificates. In addition, in El Salvador, individuals have two surnames, and on Helena's birth certificate, one of her mother's surnames was listed, while on her sister's birth certificate, the other surname appeared. The paralegal advised Helena that without another official document that listed both of her mother's surnames, officials might not believe that she and her sister were related.

8. AEF 2018a, 1.

9. AEF 2018a, 1.

10. AEF 2018a, 1.

11. AEF 2018b, referencing United Nations General Assembly 1989.

12. AEF 2018b, 4; see also United Nations General Assembly 1989, Article 8.

13. Hague Convention 1993; Duncan 1993. See also discussion of Sweden's support for clean break policy in Yngvesson 2010, 78–81.

14. Modell 1994, 2; Yngvesson 2010, 43.

15. AEF 2018b, 2.

16. Sara Nordin, interview, conducted by Barbara in Stockholm on August 22, 1999; for more details on AEF and Swedish adoptions, see Yngvesson 2010.

17. For more detailed discussion of interviews with Swedish adoptees from Ethiopia, see Yngvesson 2010.

18. This complex dynamic of visibility is suggested in an interview conducted by Anna von Melen with Annelie, a woman adopted from South Korea and raised by adoptive parents in Sweden. Noting that she took comfort in her "Korean appearance," Annelie explained:

A Korean appearance is not connected to refugees. If one sees an Iranian, one thinks immediately, "refugee." Everyone who sees me understands that I am adopted, or a voluntary immigrant who works and does her part. That can feel really nice, because otherwise one is standing in a sense outside. *I feel uncomfortable in the proximity of immigrants, which I think is because in some sense they unsettle the picture I have formed of myself as Swedish. They remind me that I, too, am a kind of immigrant, even though I feel that I am not, because I don't want to see things that way.* Today I can handle it. It was worse ten years ago, when immigrants first began coming to Skellefteå [the town she lived in, in northern Sweden]. (Von Melen 1998, 163; emphasis added)

19. McDonald 2016; Jordan 2020.

20. Iser 1993, 1.

21. For example, a story in the *Los Angeles Times* described the experience of a US border patrol officer who thought he was a US citizen, only to discover that he was actually born in Mexico, making his US citizenship illusory. See Hennessy-Fiske 2019.

22. On shimmering, see Coutin 2007. On psychoanalytical notions of as-if phenomena, see Rose (1996, 9), citing Weber (1968, 14), who is referring to the subjective interpretation of action by the sociologist as involving meanings "in the minds of individual persons, partly as of something actually existing, partly as something with normative authority" as would be the case with such concepts as "the state" or other similar abstract collectivities. Weber argues that treating such social collectivities as if they were individual persons is convenient or "even indispensable" for juristic purposes, but that this approach cannot inform the work of the sociologist approaching such collectivities. And see Annelise Riles's observation in a discussion of collateral knowledge: "The very point of a legal fiction such as collateral is to place limits on reality, or rather *to draw a line between legal forms of reality and other forms of reality.* What is unique about legal knowledge is its own claims to be unique, set apart, collateral. Perhaps what we need in order to understand the generative power of the law in real-world sites like the financial markets, ironically, is less commitment to the Real. Law is out of touch with reality, as the critics routinely tell us, and that is precisely, if counterintuitively, its promise" (2011, 25; emphasis added).

23. Ngai 2004, 5.

24. Coutin 2001; Yngvesson 2000, 2002.

25. Wagner 1981, 13.

26. Wagner 1981, 12.

27. Jackson 1990.

28. Jackson 1990, 14.

29. Jackson 1990, 14.

30. Bateson 2002, 63.

31. Bateson 2002, 64.

32. Bateson 1958.

33. We are indebted to an anonymous reviewer of this manuscript for pointing out the relevance of Niklas Luhmann's work to our project. We note the overlaps between Luhmann's approach to observation (an approach that was influenced by his reading of mathematician George Spencer-Brown's *Laws of Form* 1972) and Gregory Bateson's (2002, 123) approach to binocular vision as a form of double description that provides "news of difference" or "information about 'things' in quotes, always in quotes" for an observer or seer. In a similar way, as Eva M. Knodt notes in her insightful "Foreword" to Luhmann's *Social Systems*, Luhmann focuses on the key role of an observer

who cuts up reality in a certain way in order to make it observable. . . . Reality as such, the unity of the observing system and its environment, the paradoxical sameness of difference, of inside and outside, remains inaccessible; it is what 'one does not perceive when one perceives it, "the blind spot" that enables the system to observe but escapes observation. . . . *Difference is both irreducible and paradoxical: without distinctions there would be no observable reality, yet reality itself knows no distinctions.* (Knodt 1995, xxxiv)

34. Cox 2015, 10.
35. Cox 2015, 9–10.
36. Cox 2015, 8.
37. Mahmood 2005, 199.
38. Williams 1991, 7–8.
39. Winnicott 1971; see also Williams (1991, 130) for a discussion of "multivalent ways of seeing."
40. Winnicott 1971, 2, 100.
41. Phillips 1988, 47.
42. Gilder 2008.
43. See Einstein, Podalsky, and Rosen 1935, in which the position against "spooky action at a distance" was laid out, although that phrase is never mentioned in the oft-quoted article. The phrase does appear in a letter written by Einstein to his close friend and colleague Max Born in 1947 (Born 2005, 155). See also Boughn 2018 for a more recent argument opposing the concept of spooky action. While this (entanglement) dimension of quantum physics was not initially emphasized, entanglement has become increasingly crucial in theoretical discussions and experimental physics and technology from the end of the twentieth century up to the present, as elaborated in Louisa Gilder's 2008 account. See also Rovelli 2021 for a more recent discussion of entanglement as "the radical interdependence of things" (89), an interdependence that is established in correlations between different forms of information about the world. As Rovelli explains: "A single equation codes quantum theory. It implies that the world is not continuous but granular. There is no infinite in going toward the small: things cannot get infinitely smaller. It tells us that the future is not determined by the present. It tells us that physical things have properties only in relation to other physical things and that these properties make sense only when things interact. It tells us that sometimes perspectives cannot be juxtaposed" (108–9).
44. Winnicott 1971, 107.
45. See Hull 2012; Riles 2006; Vismann 2008; Dery 1998.
46. Jackson 1990.
47. Lawrance and Stevens 2017.
48. Abarca and Coutin 2018; Ordoñez 2016; Horton and Heyman 2020; Muñiz 2019. It is ironic that when documentation is deemed potentially fraudulent, the solution is often to seek additional documentation, as when US immigration officials send requests for evidence in response to applications for regularization.
49. See discussion of adoptee birth certificates as a form of laundering that makes the adoptive family complete in Coutin, Maurer, and Yngvesson (2002, 823). Similar issues of suspicion and negation are experienced by US citizens who were born to undocumented parents and were delivered near the border, by midwives rather than by a doctor in a hospital. Such citizens' birth certificates may be viewed with suspicion by US authorities, leading to denials of passports or other documentation of nationality (Seif 2018).
50. As this discussion suggests, there are connections between our interest in documentation as a form of entanglement and recent work on the ontological turn in anthropology. This turn moves away from seeing realities as already existing in the world, only to be discovered and studied by ethnographers, to instead focusing on how seeming realities come into being (Barad 2007; Alberti et al. 2011, 904–5; Escobar 2008; Thomas 2016; M. Wright 2015). Like other anthropologists who have been influenced by this turn, we are interested more in the shifting grounds that underpin the process of becoming

than on presumed foundational distinctions between a physical world and accounts of that world. By bringing together Bateson's ecological thinking, quantum theory's approach to entanglement, and Winnicott's understanding of object relations, we explore not only how ethnographic subjects come to be but also the entanglements that make documenting such becomings possible.

51. Menjívar 2006, 1008.

52. Regarding indefinite waiting, see Andersson 2014; Hasselberg 2016; Mountz et al. 2002. Regarding the ambiguity of being both yet neither, see Hondagneu-Sotelo and Avila 1997; Zavella 2011.

53. Du Bois (1903) 2016, 10.

54. Anzaldúa 2012, 99.

55. United States v. Texas, 579 U.S. ___ 2016.

56. From a legal standpoint, a better strategy might be for the oldest child to petition for both parents upon turning twenty-one.

57. In fact, the criminal record of the person filing the petition is not at issue. It is the beneficiary of the petition who must have a clean criminal record.

58. Note that these requirements have changed and Margarita may be describing an experience that occurred before undocumented immigrants were eligible for Medi-Cal coverage. See Cha and McConville 2021 for a report that provides historical background.

59. Reminiscent of Allaine Cerwonka's comment about her time spent observing a police station in Australia: "I act like a researcher with my recorder" (Cerwonka and Malkki 2007, 120).

60. Strathern 1999, 10–11.

61. Strathern 1999, 11.

62. Heidegger 1962, 319.

63. Simmel 1990, 76.

64. Bruner 1986, 13.

65. On ethnography and dislocation, see Gupta and Ferguson 1997. On the emotional impacts of fieldwork, see Behar 2014; Visweswaran 1994.

66. Coutin, Maurer, and Yngvesson 2002.

67. See Schrödinger 1935; Le Guin 1982.

68. Yngvesson and Coutin 2008.

69. Yngvesson and Coutin 2006, 178.

70. In her nuanced account of the birth of quantum physics in the first decades of the twentieth century, Louisa Gilder (2008, 102) explores the powerful role of "*gedanken*" (or thought experiments) in what Einstein referred to as the "thought-kitchens" of an elite group of quantum theorists residing in Europe and, eventually, in the United States, where key figures immigrated to in the 1920s and 1930s. For example, describing the "progress of a sort" he had made in attempting to solve the mysteries of quantum theory in the winter of 1926, Werner Heisenberg recalled, "Coming nearer and nearer to the real thing, only to see that the paradoxes . . . got worse and worse because they turned out more clearly—that was the exciting thing. . . . Like a chemist, who tries to concentrate the poison more and more from some kind of solution, we tried to concentrate the poison of the paradox." Interview with Werner Heisenberg, 1963, in Pais 1991, 302, quoted in Gilder (2008, 102). And see Barad's (2007, 288) discussion of "gedanken, or thought, experiments" as "imagined experiments used to focus on the crucial aspects of a particular problem." See also our discussion in chapter 3 of Schrödinger's celebrated thought experiment involving the cat paradox.

71. See Yngvesson 2013, 354–64; Coutin 2016, 198–99.

72. Note that the term "rendering" here suggests an active process of extraction in which a memory may have the potential for yielding a number of possible meanings at

different times. And see Anna Gibbs's (2010, 193–94) discussion of rendering as an effect of "action on bodies (or, more accurately, on aspects of bodies). . . . It represents the organization or communication of relationships . . . through temporary captures of form by way of mimesis. Not reducible to bit units, information of this kind is a 'life process whereby difference [or pattern, relationship] is discovered in the environment.'"

73. For Schindele's innovative approach to theorizing her relationship to her country and family of birth, see Schindele 2022.

74. On ways that memory is invented, see Loftus 1993.

75. Barrett 2021, 10.

76. Barrett 2021, 10.

77. Stern 2004, 7. See also Stern (1985, 53–59) for a discussion of "vitality affects": "For example, a 'rush' of anger or of joy, a perceived flooding of light, an accelerating sequence of thoughts, an unmeasurable wave of feeling evoked by music, and a shot of narcotics can all feel like 'rushes.' They all share similar envelopes of neural firings, although in different parts of the nervous system. The felt quality of any of these similar changes is what I call the vitality affect of a 'rush'" (55–56).

78. Stern 2004, 27.

79. The "P" in the title stands for "Program" on Swedish radio.

80. Wallenstein 2021. This is a direct translation from the Swedish radio program. Wallensteen's use of mixed pronouns is because she was including herself in the assembled students. Thus she is simultaneously observer and observed. The italics are to acknowledge her own verbal emphasis of the italicized words.

81. See also Jacques Lacan (1977, 50): "The unconscious is that chapter of my history that is marked by a blank or occupied by a falsehood: it is the censored chapter. But the truth can be rediscovered; usually it has been written down elsewhere. Namely:

—in monuments: this is my body . . .

—in archival documents: these are my childhood memories . . .

—and lastly, in the traces that are inevitably preserved by the distortions necessitated by the linking of the adulterated chapter to the chapters surrounding it, and whose meaning will be established by my exegesis."

82. Coutin 2016, 4; see also Farmer 1996 and our discussion of technologies of forgetting and the archiving of memory in chapter 4.

83. Our discussion here draws from Coutin 2016, 7.

84. Gordon 1997, xvi.

85. Gordon 1997, 22.

86. Gordon 1997, 22.

87. See Cox 2015; Mahmood 2005.

88. See Le Guin 1982.

89. This image of the body as nothing more than electricity suggests that people are and are not there at the same time, that corporeal existence is something of an illusion. We discuss the indeterminacy of presence further in chapters 3 and 4.

90. Transcribed by authors from a recording of the play posted at http://howlround .com/livestreaming-performance-of-the-service-workers-project-contra-la-corriente -against-the-current, accessed September 13, 2016. Translation (by authors):

Electricity is a powerful thing. Peligrosa. Si no está controlada. [Dangerous. If it is not controlled.] Nowadays we have found ways to control it, use it for all kinds of functions. Está alrededor de nosotros. [It is all around us.] Pulsating like, like an electric heartbeat. It courses through every inch of this building. Está aquí. En estas paredes. [It is here. In these walls.] Underneath our feet. Y sobre nuestras cabezas. Algunos dicen que nuestro cuerpo no es nada más que electricidad. [And above our heads. Some say that our body is nothing more than electricity.] There are some spaces in this world where an electric current travels between a piece of metal no thicker than a sheet of paper. Sometimes that thin sheet of metal just can't take all that energy. And it burns. Se desintegra. [It disintegrates.] Disappears into nothing. La energía no puede recorrer sobre nada. [Energy cannot travel along nothing.] When that happens, lights go out. Máquinas se detienen. [Machines stop.] Stillness.

91. In chapter 2, we further discuss the relationship between disappearance and visibility.

92. Winnicott describes "*the experience* of relating to objects" with the metaphor of "electricity" (1971, 98; emphasis in original). He compares this experience of relating to "the tremendous significance that there can be in the interplay of the edges of two curtains, or of the surface of a jug that is place in front of another jug" (citing Milner 1969).

93. Our translation:

Hay cientos de edificios en esta Universidad. [There are hundreds of buildings in this University.] In each room, there are corners. El lugar en donde dos paredes se unen. [The place where two walls meet.] Corners are often the place where the most amount of dirt gathers. Muchos no se fijen en las esquinas. [Most don't pay attention to the corners.] Most don't pay attention to the nooks and crannies of a building. But the workers understand that the most important places to clean are corners, the small space where two walls meet. There are thousands of them hidden in plain sight. Like those thoughts that everyone has but won't say.

94. See García 2014.

95. Such essential workers are sometimes sacrificed due to health-care disparities. See Sanchez 2020.

2. FIELDSIGHT

1. Williams 1991, 121.

2. Williams 1991, 130; see also Anzaldúa 2012.

3. Zuberi and Bonilla-Silva 2008; Said 1979.

4. Smith 2012, 2.

5. See Iser's (1993, 148) discussion of Vaihinger's (1952, 100–101) examination of fictions as "transit points" or "hinges" between "individual sensations . . . and phenomena"; see also Winnicott 1971.

6. Iser 1993.

7. Winnicott 1971, 107.

8. Smith 2012, 5. Similarly, Gloria Anzaldúa (2012, 104) describes what she calls "the *Mestiza* way," namely a process of sorting through, analyzing, and discarding colonial or oppressive influences. She writes that the *Mestiza* "puts history through a sieve, winnows out the lies, looks at the forces that we as a race, as women, have been part of. *Luego bota lo que no vale*."

9. Boellstorff et al. 2012.

10. Haddon 1935.

11. Boyer, Faubion, and Marcus 2015.

12. See Nader 1972; Gusterson 2017; Lederman 2006; Smith 2012.

13. Cerwonka and Malkki 2007, 96, quoting Passaro 1997, 153; see also Smith 2012. In a classic article, Raymond L. Gold (1958, 220) warns that a researcher "may 'go native,' incorporate the role into his self-conceptions and achieve self-expression in the role, but find he has so violated his observer role that it is almost impossible to report his findings.

Consequently, the field worker needs cooling-off periods during and after complete participation, at which times he can 'be himself' and look back on his field behavior dispassionately and sociologically."

14. Coutin 2005; Yngvesson and Coutin 2008. See also Spencer-Brown's (1972, v) discussion of how "a universe comes into being when a space is severed or taken apart" (quoted in Watson 2020, 163).

15. Klawans 2016, 2.

16. Ombres 2014, 3.

17. Ombres 2014, 2.

18. Ombres 2014, 3.

19. Ombres 2014, 2.

20. Ombres 2014, 3.

21. Klawans 2016, 1.

22. Ombres 2014, 2.

23. Iser 1993, 79–80, referencing Nietzsche 1977, 1172.

24. Talu 2016, 9; emphasis added.

25. Bateson 2002, 65.

26. Bateson 2002, 124, 126.

27. Bateson 1958.

28. Talu 2016, 9, quoting Rosi.

29. Winnicott 1971, 2, 105, 3.

30. Winnicott 1971, 10. Winnicott also notes,

> The important part [of his concept of potential space and the location of playing] is that whereas inner psychic reality has a kind of location in the mind or in the belly or in the head or somewhere within the bounds of the individual's personality, and whereas what is called external reality is located outside those bounds, playing and cultural experience can be given a location if one uses the concept of the potential space between the mother and the baby. In the development of various individuals, it has to be recognized that the third area of potential space between mother and baby is extremely valuable according to the experiences of the child or adult who is being considered. (1971, 53)

31. Winnicott 1971, 40. See also Bateson's insightful analysis of play as a "psychological frame" or "metamessage" that signals to participants the as-if dimension in light of which an evolving series of interactions is to be understood, and the role of paradox in disturbing the dynamic interplay of figure and ground or map and territory, complicating the meaning of the interactions and the seeming solidity of the forms that materialize in their course (1972, 177–93, particularly 191–93). We engage with Bateson's analysis of play as metamessage in chapter 3.

32. Sekkel 2016, 92. Winnicott explains this complex relationship of the internal to the external, and the role of the psychologist in documenting it: "Psychologically the infant takes from a breast that is part of the infant, and the mother gives milk to an infant that is part of herself. *In psychology, the idea of interchange is based on an illusion in the psychologist*" (1971, 12; emphasis added).

33. Bateson 2002, 90.

34. Bateson 2002, 92; emphasis added.

35. Iser 1993, 92.

36. Winnicott 1971, 98.

37. Anzaldúa 2012, 99.

38. Cantú and Hurtado 2012, 7.

39. Du Bois 2016, 10. Gloria Anzaldúa's understanding of borderlands and *mestiza* consciousness draw on Du Bois's theorization. In their introduction to *Borderlands/ La Frontera*, Cantú and Hurtado (2012, 7) explain Anzaldúa's notion of "la facultad" (ability or gift)—"the notion that individuals (primarily women) who are exposed to multiple social worlds . . . develop the agility to navigate and challenge monocultural and monolingual conceptions of social reality."

40. For a more detailed discussion of Sofia Berzelius's experiences of return, see Yngvesson 2010, 116–17, 144–45.

41. Winnicott 1971, 109.

42. Winnicott 1971, 11.

43. Winnicott 1971, 12–13.

44. Grünewald 1980, 3, freely translated by Barbara Yngvesson.

45. Grünewald 1980, 4.

46. For a more detailed discussion of this event, see Yngvesson 2010, 112–13.

47. See also Abarca and Coutin 2018.

48. See Nancy (1993: 43–44) " The origin of 'abandonment' is a putting at *bandon*. *Bandon* (*bandum, band, bannen*) is an order, a prescription, and the power that holds these freely at its disposal. To *abandon*, is to remit, entrust, or turn over to such a sovereign power, and to remit, entrust, or turn over to its *ban*, that is, to its proclaiming, to its convening, and to its sentencing."

49. Rovelli (2021, 77) points out that "in our everyday life we are not aware of any of this [the properties that objects have in relation to other objects]. Quantum interference gets lost in the buzz of the macroscopic world. We can reveal it only through delicate observations, isolating objects as much as possible." Similarly, Anzaldúa (2012, 108) suggests that white people also have dual consciousnesses: "Your dual consciousness splits off parts of yourself, transferring the 'negative' parts onto us. (Where there is persecution of minorities, there is shadow projection. Where there is violence and war, there is repression of shadow.) . . . Gringo accept the doppelganger in your psyche."

50. This notion of bringing together disparate realities to produce a messier whole is developed by legal scholar Margaret Montoya through a metaphor of braiding. Montoya (1994, 187) writes of "the braiding together of the personal with the academic voice, legal scholarship with scholarship from other disciplines, narrative with expository prose and poetry, and English with Spanish. Though untidy ('grenas'), these linguistic and conceptual braids ('trenzas') challenge conventional paradigms within the legal academy and subvert the dominant discourse."

51. We return to our discussion of continuity-contiguity moments that disrupt the distinctions on which conventional realities are based in chapter 4.

52. Cox 2015, ix.

53. Cox 2015, 28.

54. Cox 2015, 62.

55. Cox 2015, 78.

56. Cox 2015, 5.

57. Cox 2015, 198. Similarly, Anzaldúa (2012, 100) writes of "the coming together of two self-consistent but habitually incompatible frames of reference." This notion of internal self-consistence combining with habitual incompatibility captures the sorts of impossible realities that are the focus of our discussion.

58. Cox 2015, 29.

59. Cox 2015, 32, citing Madison 2007.

60. Cox 2015, viii–ix.

61. Williams 1991.

62. See also Montoya 1994.

63. Williams, 1991, 7–8.

64. Williams 1991, 150.

65. Williams 1991, 163.

66. Smith 2012, 199.

67. Stone-Cadena and Álvarez Velasco 2018.

68. Stone-Cadena and Álvarez Velasco 2018, 200.

69. Stone-Cadena and Álvarez Velasco 2018, 208.

70. Nordin 1996, 4–5.

71. See Yngvesson (2000, 192–99) for a discussion of this issue.

72. It should be emphasized that adult adoptees were not alone in pressing for the acknowledgment of the birth mother as a key figure (however her presence might be realized in practice) in the Swedish adoptive family (see, for example, Stjerna 1976); but this position was not widely promoted in Sweden, unlike in the United States, where open adoptions involving contact between birth and adoptive families have long had some traction.

73. See, for example, Nordin 1996; Trotzig 1996; von Melen 1998; Wallensteen 2000, 2021; Lindqvist and Ohlén 2003; Hübinette 2004, 2006; Winkvist 2006; Hübinette and Lundström 2015; Karim 2017; Schindele 2022.

74. For a more detailed discussion of the Forum '97 workshops, see Yngvesson 2010, 123–27. See also Bateson's (2002, 116) discussion of "the essence of play" as lying "in a partial denial of the meanings that the actions would have had in other situations."

75. Swedish researchers produced a number of scientific studies, beginning in the 1990s, documenting problems of adaptation and adjustment among transnational adoptees. A more comprehensive set of studies appeared in the early 2000s documenting the high rate of mental health disturbances—including depression, drug abuse, and notably suicide—in the cohort of transnational adoptees adopted in 1970 as compared with control groups consisting of immigrant youths, native-born Swedes, and the native-born siblings of transnational adoptees who were born in the same period. Particularly powerful in some of these studies was an ideological mindset that viewed adopted children as the embodiment of so-called early disturbances that continued to affect their well-being as they matured in spite of the efforts of loving adoptive parents. See, for example, Cederblad et al. 1994, 1999; Hjern and Allbeck 2002; Hjern, Lindblad, and Vinnerljung 2002; Lindqvist and Ohlén 2003. For a critical perspective on "early disturbances" among Swedish transnational adoptees, see Yngvesson (2010, 105–22) and the documentary film *De Ensamma* (Karim 2017).

76. Bateson 1972, 181.

77. Ombres 2014.

78. Talu 2016, 8; emphasis added.

79. Talu, 2016, 5.

80. Talu 2016, 5.

81. Talu 2016, 6; emphasis added.

82. Talu 2016, 5; see also Rony 1996 for an insightful discussion of the third eye in ethnographic film.

83. Ombres 2014, 3.

84. Bateson 1958, 280.

85. Ombres 2014, 3.

3. SCHRÖDINGER'S CAT

1. This chapter is based on Yngvesson and Coutin 2008.

2. Geertz, for example, writes that "fictions" are "something made" not something false (1973, 15). See also Clifford and Marcus 1986; Marcus and Fischer 1986.

3. Examples of such retroactive instantiations on the part of interlocuters include Kanthi's realization during her visit to the Kolkata orphanage when she was ten years old that she and the child who remained in the orphanage were "the same child"; or the realization of Diana, an unauthorized Mexican immigrant, that undocumented women could simultaneously be in downtown LA and in a hole in the ground, as described in chapter 2.

4. Sekkel 2016, 92; see also Jackson 1990, 14.

5. Of course, ethnographic knowledge can play a deeply problematic role in power relations, and in these cases, the impact of ethnography may not be significantly different from law. See McFate 2005 for a detailed history of anthropology's relationship to counterinsurgency, and Smith 2012 for an account of how research can be decolonized.

6. Greene 2005, 179. Greene also notes, "[Richard] Feynman called this the *sum over histories* approach to quantum mechanics; it shows that a probability wave embodies all possible pasts that could have preceded a given observation, and illustrates well that to succeed where classical physics failed, quantum mechanics had to substantially broaden the framework of history" (180).

7. Schrödinger 1935; see also Nadeau and Kafatos 1999, 56–59.

8. Greene 2005, 179.

9. "There is now overwhelming evidence for this so-called *quantum entanglement*. If two photons are entangled, the successful measurement of either photon's spin about one axis 'forces' the other, more distant photon to have the same spin about the same axis; the act of measuring one photon 'compels' the other, possibly distant photon to snap out of the haze of probability and take on a definitive spin value—a value that precisely matches the spin of its distant companion. And that boggles the mind" (Greene 2005, 115).

10. Waldron 1995, 193.

11. Waldron 1995,194.

12. Of course, regardless of the legal erasure of giving birth, birth mothers and birth children may continue to regard birth as a real event. The persistence of these social definitions of birth (and of potential alternative legal meanings) is one of the factors that compel searches for origins and efforts to bridge the gaps created by erasure.

13. Strathern 1999, 5.

14. Bateson 1972, 74.

15. Bateson 1972, 75.

16. Bateson 1972, 74.

17. Bateson 1972, 75.

18. Bateson 1958, 175; emphasis in original. In this context, Bateson described the status quo "as a dynamic equilibrium, in which changes are continually taking place. On the one hand, processes of differentiation tending towards increase of the ethological contrast, and on the other, processes which continually counteract this tendency towards differentiation." Bateson argued that such processes of differentiation, which he referred to by the term "schismogenesis," should be considered as having "very wide sociological and psychological significance" (1958, 175).

19. Bateson 1958, 281.

20. Bateson 1958, 259.

21. Bateson 1958, 260; emphasis in original.

22. Bateson 1958, 200.

23. Bateson 1958, 200–201.

24. Bateson 2002, 133.

25. Bateson 1958, 260.

26. Bateson 2002, 182; emphasis in original.

27. E. Wright, 2008, 15. Bateson (2002) conceptualized play as a "manipulation of frames" that involves binocular vision and has the potential for precipitating paradox.

Bateson, like Winnicott and Rosi, is interested in "the subject of boundaries" (123) and particularly in exploring the concept of relationship as "not internal to the single person" but *always a product of double description*" (124). Like Winnicott, Bateson developed his understanding of the productivity of boundaries and their manipulation in the materialization of an "interpersonal field" through observations of children's play (in Bateson's case, the observations took place during fieldwork in Bali). Wolfgang Iser (1993, 247–250), in a discussion of Bateson's theorization of play, and specifically of the potential for creative manipulation of the map-territory (or signifier/signified) relationship in the context of play, points to the productivity of Bateson's understanding of "the paradox of a difference [between map and territory] that is simultaneously removed and preserved," since "the signifier stands under the proviso of the 'as-if': it has been uncoupled from its conventional code" (249).

28. Bateson 2002, 130; emphasis in original.

29. Bateson 1972, 191; see also Winnicott 1971.

30. Bateson 2002, 130.

31. Bateson 2002, 130.

32. Bateson 1972, 183.

33. Bateson 1972, 187.

34. Bateson 1958, 74.

35. Bateson 1958, 35.

36. Conrad 2012, 209; see also Yngvesson 2013, 335.

37. Probyn 1996, 35.

38. Bateson 1972, 42.

39. Bateson 1958, 280.

40. Bateson 2002, 134; see also discussion of abduction or lateral extension in this chapter.

41. For a critique of the politics of comparison, see Stoler 2010.

42. Coutin, Maurer, and Yngvesson 2002.

43. Yngvesson and Coutin 2006.

44. See, for example, our discussion in chapter 2 of Gregory Bateson's insightful observations about the two-eyed method of seeing, and its implications for the way "we *draw* distinctions, that is, we *pull* them out" of events "that correspond to *outlines* in the visible world" (2002, 90).

45. Cox 2015, 9–10. One example of such an extreme situation was Kim Fortun's 2001 study of the Bhopal disaster, which threw conventional understandings of instrumental data collection into disarray, producing a "barrage of data" (348).

46. Strathern 1999, 10.

47. Benjamin 1968, 75.

48. See discussion in chapter 2 of Katarina, another unauthorized US immigrant interviewed by Coutin, who described her experience of inhabiting a world in which her social location and jurisdictional status did not coincide: "There is nothing here, there is nothing there," and "you're just walking around, and you're just, you're like invisible to everything else."

49. Žižek 1989, 18.

50. Latour 1999, 64. Latour describes this process (borrowing a term from semiotics) as "shifting (in, out, down)" (310–11). As a result of this process, an "internal" referent, or depth of vision (here, now, I; there, then, he or she) is constituted. This "internal" realm, as Simmel noted almost a century ago, is neither subjective nor objective but arises from "the practical relation between man and his object," a relation that combines both proximity (desire) and distance (value) for its realization (1990, 77). See also Appadurai 1986, 3–6.

51. See Greenhouse 1996.

52. Greene 2005, 185.
53. See also Coutin et al. 2002.
54. Latour 1999, 310.
55. Latour 1999,76.
56. Liem 2000.
57. On framing, see Heidegger (1978) 1993. In addition, as Bourdieu (1987, 233–34) notes,

> The judgment [of a court] represents the quintessential form of authorized, public, official speech which is spoken in the name of and to everyone. These performative utterances, substantive—as opposed to procedural—decisions publicly formulated by authorized agents acting on behalf of the collectivity, are magical acts which succeed because they have the power to make themselves universally recognized. They thus succeed in creating a situation in which no one can refuse or ignore the point of view, the vision, which they impose. . . . It would not be excessive to say that [law] *creates* the social world, but only if we remember that it is this world which first creates the law.

58. Strathern 1999, 10.
59. Latour 1999, 69.
60. Latour 1999, 71.
61. Latour 1999, 73.
62. This recalls the discussion in Callon et al. (2002, 199) of the process of qualification in which goods are produced and stabilized.
63. See, for example, Trotzig 1996; Aronson 1997; Trenka 2003, 2009; Hubinette 2004; Kim 2010; Knowlton 2011; Boileau and Henin 2013; Karim 2017; Liem 2018; Johnson 2018; Sjöblom 2019; Schindele 2022.
64. Anderson and Solis 2014.
65. Fortun 2001, 348.
66. Le Guin 1982.
67. Le Guin 1982, 48–49.

4. THE SEARCH FOR A "BACK"

1. For Winnicott (1971, 90–91), the process of making an object (the mother, an Other more generally) real is inseparable from a process of destruction, in which the object of fantasy (of internal reality) is destroyed but survives the destruction. See also Phillips (1988): "*It is destructiveness, paradoxically, that creates reality, not reality that creates destructiveness*" (132; emphasis added); and "Vitality and the sense of being really alive are clearly bound up for him [Winnicott] with the aggressive component" (111).
2. Winnicott 1971, 103; Sekkel 2016, 92.
3. Quotations from *Nostalgia for the Light* are the authors' translation of Spanish excerpts they transcribed from the film.
4. Winnicott 1971, 104.
5. Winnicott 1971, 3; emphasis in original. Winnicott notes that "Madness here simply means a *break-up* of whatever may exist at the time of *a personal continuity of existence*" (1971, 97; emphasis in original). A recent example is provided by Katarina, a woman interviewed in a documentary film about Swedish transracial adoptees by Osmond Karim, *De Ensamma* (2017). Adopted from Colombia by Swedish parents, Katarina describes the experience of meeting her birth mother in Colombia, after the birth of her own fourth child in Sweden, as opening up "all kinds of feelings—like being completely in love—with my own mother. It was even physical. I was like a child. It was a regression. I just wanted to lie next to her. . . . It was just: 'I need this.'"

6. The quotations in this section are from an interview Barbara conducted with Berzelius in August 2002 in Stockholm.

7. "I'd like to stop searching and just BE. Yes, looking-for is evidence that there is a self" (words of a patient, quoted in Winnicott 1971, 63).

8. Winnicott 1971, 11.

9. See Rose (1996, 5): "Like blood, fantasy is thicker than water, all too solid—*contra* another of fantasy's more familiar glosses as ungrounded supposition, lacking in foundation, not solid *enough*. For one line of thinking, the concepts of state and fantasy are more or less antagonists, back to back, facing in opposite directions towards public and private worlds. But fantasy, even on its own psychic terms, is never only inwardly-turning; it always contains a historical reference in so far as it involves, alongside the attempt to arrest the present, a journey through the past."

10. Sekkel 2016, 86; Benjamin 1968, 255.

11. Or as when the novelist Hisham Matar (2016, 108) encountered the light of Benghazi: "The Benghazi light is a material. You can almost feel its weight, the way it falls and holds its subject."

12. Ombres 2014, 3.

13. Matar 2016, 47–48; emphasis added.

14. This young astronomer's description of the interrelationship of the universe and human lives is reminiscent of Bateson's ecological thinking, discussed in chapter 2.

15. Matar 2016, 24.

16. Khosravi 2010, 74.

17. Khosravi 2010, 74

18. Derrida 1996.

19. Ketelaar 2001, 138; see also Cook 2001.

20. Posocco 2011, 452.

21. Weld 2014, 87.

22. Weld 2014, 197.

23. Weld 2014, 150. Later, when relatives of the disappeared migrated to places like the United States and applied for asylum, their inability to identify these plainclothes officers could be held against them—how could applicants credibly claim that they were in danger from the state if they didn't know who was responsible for perpetrating abuses?

24. Weld 2014, 163.

25. Bateson 1972, 180.

26. As Jaqueline Rose (1996, 52) notes, "Identification relies on spots of blindness—one link recognized, another immediately put back beyond memory, pushed underground."

27. Lautaro Núñez, quoted in Gúzman, *Nostalgia for the Light.*

28. Mountz et al. 2002; Hasselberg 2016; Andersson 2014.

29. Matar 2016, 23; emphasis added.

30. Weld 2014, 125.

31. Weld 2014, 166.

32. Simmel 1990, 81.

33. "Yo no *podría* olvidar, yo tendría la obligación ética de recoger esa memoria. Es imposible olvidar nuestros muertos. Hay que mantenerlos en la memoria."

34. Fortun 2012, 455. See also our discussion of Anzaldúa's (2012, 99) concept of a "new *mestiza* consciousness" in chapter 1.

35. Sekkel 2016, 88.

36. Sekkel 2016, 88, describing Winnicott.

37. See our discussion in chapter 1 of psychologist Daniel Stern's (2004, 7) concept of the "present moment" as "the passing moment in which something happens as time

unfolds. It is the coming into being of a new state of things, and it happens in a moment of awareness.... It is a small window of becoming and opportunity." See also Walter Benjamin's (1968, 255) discussion of "seizing" the past "as an image which flashes up at the instant when it can be recognized and is never seen again."

38. Gaspar Galasz, quoted in *Nostalgia*. See also Coutin's (2013, 113) discussion of law as a material force that "derives from rather than exists in spite of moments when law is rendered illusory."

39. Matar 2016, 145.

40. Matar 2016, 145.

41. Matar 2016, 31.

42. Iser 1993, 295, drawing on Husserl 1980, 80–81.

43. Matar 2016, 104.

44. Iser 1993, 16.

45. Matar 2016, 158. In this passage, Matar is referring both to Manet's *The Execution of Maximilian*, which "evokes the inconclusive fate of my father and the men who died in Abu Salim," and to Titian's *The Martyrdom of Saint Lawrence*, which he saw at an exhibition in Rome a few days after his return to Libya. Titian's painting depicts Lawrence pinned to a bench, beneath which a fire has been built. "There is no end to Lawrence's torment. He is surrounded by efficient men" (146). Matar continues:

> That day in Rome, after I had seen my country for the first time in thirty-three years, after I had found out all I could find out about what had befallen my father, I sat on the floor of the emptying gallery, looking up at *The Martyrdom of Saint Lawrence*, sketching in my notebook ... and then, without noticing that I had surrendered to them, I was surrounded by sounds and images, coming at me in sharp broken fragments, of Father's final moments: what they might have told him, what his last words might have been, the past and how it seemed to him then. (147)

46. Matar 2016, 124–25; emphasis added.

47. Bateson 2002, 133; see also chapter 3 in this book. Bateson's use of the term "abduction" suggests that perception can be pulled (as by the force of gravity) in a direction that is not governed by individual will. As a form of double description, abduction is much like the dual vantage point engendered by irresolution. Bateson's comment that "the very possibility of abduction is a little uncanny" (133) is not unlike Matar's reflection regarding his experience in switching his focus to Manet's *The Execution of Maximilian* at the National Gallery in London: "What sent a shiver through me was the fact that, on the day 1,270 men were executed in the prison where my father was held, I chose to switch my vigil" (2016, 157).

48. The phrasing here is similar to Latour's discussion, quoted in chapter 3 of this book, about how only when one reaches an origin point does the network begin to lie.

49. Matar 2016, 43.

50. Khosravi 2010, 73–74.

51. Khosravi 2010, 74.

52. Khosravi 2010, 22–23.

53. Weld 2014, 161.

54. Weld 2014, 22.

55. On labors of memory, see Jelin 2003, 6–7. The reference to bringing workers' dead back to life is from Weld 2014, 166.

56. Weld 2014, 241; emphasis added.

57. Weld 2014, 163.

58. Khosravi 2010.

59. Mbembe 2002, quoted in Weld 2014, 159.

60. Sekkel 2016, 88.

61. For instance, see Dery's (1998) notion of "papereality" and Llewellyn's (1930) discussion of "paper rules."

62. Baker-Cristales 2012, 15.

63. Sekkel 2016, 86. On fictionalizing acts, see Iser 1993.

64. Mitchell and Coutin 2019. An example of the legally cognizable certificate would be a birth certificate created for an adopted child whose original certificate has been sealed and is thus rendered invalid, even as the child's birth mother is rendered not-a-mother (see discussion in chapter 3). In such a case, the new certificate authenticates a fiction: that the adopted child is the begotten child of its adoptive parents.

65. Bateson 2002, 134; see also discussion of abduction in Matar's experience.

66. Talu 2016, 4; emphasis added; see also Schwab 2010.

67. Matar 2016, 5. Documents are not the only form of evidence. When he was in prison, Matar's father recited poetry through his cell door but did not identify himself to his imprisoned comrades. Seemingly, he desired to be recognized "without needing to provide any more evidence," perhaps hoping that if he were to be recognized, then he was still the same person (Matar 2016, 60). Matar himself feared what he would experience if he actually went into Abu Salim, where his father was killed. It would seem that echoes and recognition are part of the mystery or perhaps magic of alive-deadness.

68. Iser 1993, 295.

69. Iser 1993, 146; Vaihinger 1952.

70. Weld 2014, 163.

71. Posocco 2011, 449.

72. Jackson 1990.

73. See, for example, Posocco's (2011, 452) discussion of "an archive of *evil*," quoting Carolyn Steedman's (2009) reading of Derrida's meditation on the "*mal d'archive*": "The sickness of the archive is also and at the same time an archive of disaster and destruction; indeed (for the French *mal* does not mince its meaning) it is an archive of *evil*. Derrida [. . .] emphasizes again the institution of archives as the expression of state power."

74. Weld 2014, 155, 160.

75. Another example of doubling arises in the case of immigration, in which "noncitizens come to know the state intimately in that they seek to anticipate and thus shape its actions, even as this effort in turn shapes them" (Abarca and Coutin 2018, 8).

76. Quoted in Sandhu 2012, 2.

77. Sandhu 2012, 2.

78. Sandhu 2012, 2–3.

79. Our phrasing here echoes the title of our prologue, "What lies back of the work," a phrase taken from the anthropologist Margaret Mead's introduction to Ruth Benedict's published papers. Please see endnote 2 of the prologue for the full quote.

5. BEYOND "SPOOKY ACTION AT A DISTANCE"

1. Le Guin 2001, 1.

2. Le Guin 2001, 1.

3. Le Guin 2001, 1

4. Le Guin 2001, 3.

5. Le Guin 2001, 9.

6. Le Guin 2001, 29.

7. Le Guin 2001, 29.

8. Le Guin 2001, 29.

9. Le Guin 2001, 189.

10. See the prologue and chapter 1 for a discussion of Einstein's use of this phrase.

11. Nadeau and Kafatos 1999, 2.

12. See Mermin 1990; Gilder 2008; and Rovelli 2021; see also discussion of entanglement in chapter 1.

13. Nadeau and Kafatos 1999, 4.

14. Gefter 2014b, 298. Gefter adds, "Even though the global view is fundamentally flawed, the local causal patch measure offers us a way to still talk about a global view *as if* it actually means something" (298; emphasis added).

15. Gefter 2014b, 285.

16. Gefter 2014b, 274. The quotation is from one of the physicist John Archibald Wheeler's journals—archived at the American Philosophical Society in Philadelphia— in which he struggles with the role of observers in the creation of physical reality. Gefter quotes extensively from Wheeler's journals, notably in chapter 11 of her book, but provides neither the volume nor the page number for this quotation.

17. See Bekenstein 2003, 63–64; Cowen 2015, 291.

18. Cowen 2015, 291.

19. Cowen 2015, 291.

20. Cowen 2015, 292, citing the work of Van Raamsdonk 2010.

21. Nadeau and Kafatos note that in so-called delayed-choice experiments with single photons, the single photons "follow two paths, or one path, according to a choice made 'after' the photon has followed one or both paths" (1999, 50). See also Gefter 2014b, 104, quoting Wheeler 1996, 42, regarding delayed-choice experiments in laboratories: "Each time they've worked just as Wheeler suggested. It's an established scientific fact: measurements in the present can rewrite history. No, not rewrite. Just write. Prior to observation, there is no history, just a haze of possibility, waiting to be born. 'There is no more remarkable feature of this quantum world than the strange coupling it brings about between future and past,' Wheeler wrote." And see Rovelli 2021, 89–113 and our discussion of entanglement in chapter 1.

22. Prébin 2013, 180–81.

23. Hamner 2005, 237.

24. Hamner 2005, 237–38.

25. See Gefter 2014b, 104, quoting Wheeler 1994, 19: "'We used to think the world exists "out there" independent of us,' he said, 'we the observer, safely hidden behind a one-foot thick slab of plate glass, not getting involved, just observing. However, we've concluded in the meantime that that isn't the way the world works. In fact, we have to smash the glass, reach in.'" Quoting Rovelli (1996, 1643), Gefter (2014b, 362) underscores the key significance of Wheeler's lifelong fascination with the problem of the second observer (what Gefter describes as the problem of coauthorship and we have termed, following Bateson, double description or binocular vision):

> If different observers give different accounts of the same sequence of events, then each quantum mechanical description has to be understood as relative to a particular observer. Thus a quantum mechanical description of a certain system (state and/or values of physical quantities) cannot be taken as an "absolute" (observer-independent) description of reality, but rather as a formalization, or codification, of properties of a system *relative* to a given observer. . . . In quantum mechanics, "state" as well as "value of a variable"—or "outcome of a measurement"—are relational notions.

As Gefter (2014b, 364) summarizes Rovelli's argument: "According to Rovelli, reality itself was observer-dependent. Which meant, however insane it sounded, that reality itself *wasn't real.*"

26. See Schneider 1980; Franklin 1995, 2013; Castañeda 2002; Strathern 2005; Yngvesson and Coutin 2006; Yngvesson 2010; Rapp and Ginsburg 2011; Prébin 2013.

27. Cox 2015, 10.

28. Sekkel 2016, 92, citing Benjamin 1993.

29. Prébin 2013.

30. Prébin 2013, 179.

31. Yngvesson 2010, citing Sammarco 2003, 7.

32. Sekkel 2016, 88, citing Benjamin 1993 and Winnicott 1971.

33. Dauvergne 2008, 15.

34. Stone-Cadena and Álvarez Velasco 2018.

35. United States District Court, Southern District of California 2018.

36. Schneider 1980; Coutin, Richland, and Fortín 2014; Khosravi 2010. The example of exiles experiencing eruptions of home also brings to mind Hale's 1863 story, "The Man without a Country" (see Hale 1900).

37. Nadeau and Kafatos 1999, 50.

38. Iser 1993, 92.

39. Winnicott 1971, 2.

40. See McNally 2006.

41. This tension is evocative of Walter Benjamin's discussion of an "original language" in "The Task of the Translator," and his observation that "to some degree all great texts contain their potential translation between the lines" (1968, 82).

42. See Knodt's discussion of Spencer-Brown's *Laws of Form* and the "blind spot" that "enables the system to observe but escapes observation" (Knodt 1995, xxxiv).

43. Ngai 2004.

44. Bateson 1972, 86–87.

45. Tranströmer 1997, 136.

46. Cox 2015, 7.

47. Williams 1991.

48. Bateson 2002, 92.

49. Bateson 2002, 92.

50. Greene writes, "Back in 1687, when Newton proposed his universal law of gravity, he was actually making a strong statement about the number of space dimensions. Newton didn't just say that the force of attraction between two objects gets weaker as the distance between them gets larger. He proposed a formula, the *inverse square law*, which describes precisely how the gravitational attraction between two objects will diminish as two objects are separated" (Greene 2005, 394–95).

51. Gefter 2014a, 553.

52. Gefter 2014a, 553.

53. Gefter 2014a, 553, citing Susskind 2016, 29.

54. Gefter 2014b, 317.

55. Iser 1993, 295, citing Husserl 1980, 80–81; emphasis added.

56. Weld 2014, 163.

57. Mbembe 2002, 25, quoted in Weld 2014, 159.

58. Here we have paraphrased Amanda Gefter's (2014b, 99–10) discussion of legendary physicist John Archibald Wheeler's position, as articulated in Wheeler's journals and in his (1996) essays on physics. See also Rovelli 2021, 89–99.

59. Gefter 2014b, 7–9, 288–89.

60. Wheeler 1996, 292, quoted in Gefter 2014b, 274.

61. Gefter 2014a, 553.

62. Gefter, 2014a, 553.

63. Ellerby 2018, 11.

64. Walker 2018, 14.

65. Briggs 2018, 22. As we have pointed out, translating across the boundary established by law, a boundary between the canceled past of adoptee–birth parent and the legal present of an adoptive family, or between biological and legally established kinship, reveals that the insights of birth parents and adoptees also have bearing on the non-adopted.

66. *Escalera*, from the series *Testing Trump's Wall*, 2017, created by the visual artist Jill Marie Holslin, who was the lead artist on the series and the public art project of the same name, which was the source of this image.

67. Morrissey 2017. In an e-mail dated November 22, 2021, Holslin informed us that she was the artist quoted in this news story. See Holslin 2020 for an account of hacking the border.

References

Abarca, Gray A., and Susan Bibler Coutin. 2018. "Sovereign Intimacies: The Lives of Documents within US State-Noncitizen Relationships." *American Ethnologist* 45 (1): 7–19.

AEF (Association of Ethiopian and Eritrean Adoptees). 2018a. "Skrivelse till Sveriges Riksdag och Regering från Adopterade Etiopiers och Eritreaners förening" [Formal petition to the Swedish parliament and government from the Association of Ethiopian and Eritrean Adoptees]. Petition, Stockholm, February 13, 2018. Copy of this petition is in private collection of Barbara Yngvesson.

——. 2018b. "Upprop från Adopterade Etiopiers och Eritreaners Förening till Sveriges Riksdag och Regering" [Appeal from the Association of Ethiopian and Eritrean Adoptees to the Swedish parliament and government]. Petition, Stockholm, March 13, 2018. Copy of this appeal is in private collection of Barbara Yngvesson.

Alberti, Ben, Severin M. Fowles, Martin Holbraad, Yvonne Marshall, and Chris Whitmore. 2011. "'Worlds Otherwise': Archaeology, Anthropology, and Ontological Difference." *Current Anthropology* 52 (6): 896–912.

Anderson, Jill, and Nin Solis. 2014. *Los otros dreamers*. Mexico City: Jill Anderson & Nin Solis.

Andersson, Ruben. 2014. "Time and the Migrant Other: European Border Controls and the Temporal Economics of Illegality." *American Anthropologist* 116 (4): 795–809.

Anzaldúa, Gloria. 2012. *Borderlands: La Frontera; The New Mestiza*. 4th ed. San Francisco: Aunt Lute Books. First published 1987.

Appadurai, Arjun. 1986. "Introduction: Commodities and the Politics of Value." In *The Social Life of Things: Commodities in Cultural Perspective*, edited by Arjun Appadurai, 3–63. Cambridge: Cambridge University Press.

Arendt, Hannah. 1968. "Introduction: Walter Benjamin: 1892–1940." In *Illuminations: Essays and Reflections*, by Walter Benjamin, translated by Harry Zohn, 1–58. New York: Schocken Books.

Aronson, Jaclyn. 1997. "'Not My Homeland': A Critique of the Current Culture of Korean International Adoption." Senior thesis, Hampshire College.

Baker-Cristales, Beth. 2012. "Poiesis of Possibility: The Ethnographic Sensibilities of Ursula K. Le Guin." *Anthropology and Humanism* 37 (1): 15–26.

Barad, Karen. 2007. *Meeting the Universe Halfway: Quantum Physics and the Entanglement of Matter and Meaning*. Durham, NC: Duke University Press.

Barrett, Lisa Feldman. 2021. "How Your Mind Is Made." *MIT Technology Review* 124 (5): 8–11.

Bateson, Gregory. 1958. *Naven: A Survey of the Problems Suggested by a Composite Picture of the Culture of a New Guinea Tribe Drawn from Three Points of View*. 2nd ed. Stanford, CA: Stanford University Press. First published 1936.

——. 1972. *Steps to an Ecology of Mind*. New York: Ballantine Books.

——. 2002. *Mind and Nature: A Necessary Unity*. Cresskill, NJ: Hampton Press. First published 1979.

Behar, Ruth. 2014. *The Vulnerable Observer: Anthropology That Breaks Your Heart*. Boston: Beacon Press.

Bekenstein, Jacob D. 2003. "Information in the Holographic Universe." *Scientific American*, August 2003, 58–65. http://dx.doi.org/10.1038/scientificamerican0803-58.

Benedict, Ruth. 1959. *An Anthropologist at Work*. Edited by Margaret Mead. Cambridge: Riverside Press.

Benjamin, Walter. 1968. *Illuminations: Essays and Reflections*. Translated by Harry Zohn. New York: Schocken Books.

——. 1978. *Reflections: Essays, Aphorisms, Autobiographical Writings*. Edited by Peter Demetz. Translated by Edmund Jephcott. New York: Schocken Books.

——. 1993. "A doutrina das semelhanças" [The doctrine of similarities]. In *Obras escolhidas* vol. 1, *Magia e técnica, arte e política*. 6th ed., 108–13. Sao Paulo, SP: Brasiliense. Original study published 1933.

Boellstorff, Tom, Bonnie Nardi, Celia Pearce, T. Taylor, and George Marcus. 2012. *Ethnography and Virtual Worlds: A Handbook of Method*. Princeton, NJ: Princeton University Press.

Boileau, Laurent, and Jung Henin, dirs. 2013. *Approved for Adoption: An Animated Memoir*.

Born, Max. 2005. *The Born-Einstein Letters 1916–1955: Friendship, Politics, and Physics in Uncertain Times*. New York: Macmillan. First published in English in 1971.

Boughn, Stephen. 2018. "There Is No Action at a Distance in Quantum Mechanics, Spooky or Otherwise." Preprint, submitted June 20, 2018. https://arxiv.org/abs/1806.07925.

Bourdieu, Pierre. 1987. "The Force of Law: Toward a Sociology of the Juridical Field." *Hastings Law Journal* 38 (5): 814–53.

Boyer, Dominic, James D. Faubion, and George E. Marcus, eds. 2015. *Theory Can Be More Than It Used to Be: Learning Anthropology's Method in a Time of Transition*. Ithaca, NY: Cornell University Press.

Briggs, Laura. 2018. "Adoption, from Private to Public: Intimate Economies." *Adoption and Culture* 6 (1): 22–24.

Bruner, Jerome. 1986. *Actual Minds, Possible Worlds*. Cambridge, MA: Harvard University Press.

Callon, Michel, Cécile Meadél, and Vololona Rabeharisoa. 2002. "The Economy of Qualities." *Economy and Society* 31 (2): 194–217.

Cantú, Norma Élia, and Aída Hurtado. 2012. Introduction to *Borderlands: Law Frontera; The New Mestiza*, by Gloria Anzaldúa. 4th ed., 3–13. San Francisco: Aunt Lute Books.

Castañeda, Claudia. 2002. *Figurations: Child, Bodies, Worlds*. Durham, NC: Duke University Press.

Cederblad, Marianne, Börje Höök, Malin Irhammar, and Ann Mari Mercke. 1999. "Mental Health in International Adoptees as Teenagers and Young Adults: An Epidemiological Study." *Journal of Child Psychology and Psychiatry* 40 (8): 1239–48.

Cederblad, Marianne, Malin Irhammar, Ann Mari Mercke, and Eva Norlander. 1994. *Identitet och anpassning hos utlandsfödda adopterade ungdomar* [Identity and adjustment among foreign-born adopted youth]. Lund, Sweden: Forskning om barn och familj, Avdelning för barn och ungdomspsykiatri, Lund University.

Cerwonka, Allaine, and Liisa H. Malkki. 2007. *Improvising Theory: Process and Temporality in Ethnographic Fieldwork*. Chicago: University of Chicago Press.

Cha, Paulette, and Shannon McConville. 2021. Health Coverage and Care for Undocumented Immigrants: An Update. San Francisco: Public Policy Institute of California. https://www.ppic.org/publication/health-coverage-and-care-for-undocumented-immigrants/. Accessed February 12, 2021.

Chavez, Leo. 2013. *The Latino Threat: Constructing Immigrants, Citizens, and the Nation*. Stanford, CA: Stanford University Press.

Clifford, James, and George E. Marcus, eds. 1986. *Writing Culture: The Poetics and Politics of Ethnography*. Berkeley: University of California Press.

Congressional Research Service, 2021. *The Trump Administration's "Zero Tolerance" Immigration Enforcement Policy*. Updated February 2, 2021. https://fas.org/sgp/crs/homesec/R45266.pdf.

Conrad, Rachel. 2012. "'My Future Doesn't Know ME': Time and Subjectivity in Poetry by Young People." *Childhood* 19 (2): 204–18.

Cook, Terry. 2001. "Archival Science and Postmodernism: New Formulations for Old Concepts." *Archival Science* 1 (1): 3–24. https://doi.org/10.1007/BF02435636.

Coutin, Susan Bibler. 2001. "The Oppressed, the Suspect, and the Citizen: Subjectivity in Competing Accounts of Political Violence." *Law and Social Inquiry* 26 (1): 63–94.

——. 2005. "Being En Route." *American Anthropologist* 107 (2): 195–206.

——. 2007. *Nations of Emigrants: Shifting Boundaries of Citizenship in El Salvador and the United States*. Ithaca, NY: Cornell University Press.

——. 2013. "In the Breach: Citizenship and Its Approximations." *Indiana Journal of Global Legal Studies*, no. 20, 109.

——. 2016. *Exiled Home: Salvadoran Transnational Youth in the Aftermath of Violence*. Durham, NC: Duke University Press.

Coutin, Susan Bibler, Bill Maurer, and Barbara Yngvesson. 2002. "In the Mirror: The Legitimation Work of Globalization." *Law and Social Inquiry* 27 (4): 801–43.

Coutin, Susan Bibler, Justin Richland, and Véronique Fortín. 2014. "Routine Exceptionality: The Plenary Power Doctrine, Immigrants, and the Indigenous under US Law." *UC Irvine Law Review*, no. 4, 97–120.

Cowen, Ron. 2015. "Space, Time, Entanglement." *Nature*, no. 52, 290–93.

Cox, Aimee Meredith. 2015. *Shapeshifters: Black Girls and the Choreography of Citizenship*. Durham, NC: Duke University Press.

Dauvergne, Catherine. 2008. *Making People Illegal: What Globalization Means for Migration and Law*. Cambridge: Cambridge University Press.

De Baecque, Antoine. 2012. *Camera Historica: The Century in Cinema*. New York: Columbia University Press.

Derrida, Jacques. 1996. *Archive Fever: A Freudian Impression*. Translated by Eric Prenowitz. Chicago: University of Chicago Press.

Dery, David. 1998. "'Papereality' and Learning in Bureaucratic Organizations." *Administration and Society* 29 (6): 677–89.

Du Bois, W. E. B. (1903) 2016. *The Souls of Black Folk*. Chicago: A. C. McClurg. Reprint, New York: Dover.

Duncan, William. 1993. "Regulating Intercountry Adoption: An International Perspective." In *Frontiers of Family Law*, edited by Andrew Bainham and David S. Pearl, 46–61. New York: Wiley.

Einstein, Albert, Boris Podolsky, and Nathan Rosen. 1935. "Can Quantum-Mechanical Description of Physical Reality Be Considered Complete?" *Physical Review* 47 (10): 777–80.

Ellerby, Janet Mason. 2018. "Birthmothers: Their Rightful Place in Critical Adoption Studies." *Adoption and Culture* 6 (1): 9–11.

Escobar, Arturo. 2008. *Territories of Difference: Place, Movements, Life*. Durham, NC: Duke University Press.

Farmer, Paul. 1996. "On Suffering and Structural Violence: A View from Below." *Daedalus* 125 (1): 261–83.

Fortun, Kim. 2001. *Advocacy after Bhopal: Environmentalism, Disaster, New Global Orders*. Chicago: University of Chicago Press.

——. 2012. "Ethnography in Late Industrialism." *Cultural Anthropology* 27 (3): 446–64. https://doi.org/10.1111/j.1548-1360.2012.01153.x.

Franklin, Sarah. 1995. "Postmodern Procreation: A Cultural Account of Assisted Reproduction." In *Conceiving the New World Order: The Global Politics of Reproduction*, edited by Faye D. Ginsburg and Rayna Rapp, 323–45. Berkeley: University of California Press.

——. 2013. *Biological Relatives: IVF, Stem Cells, and the Future of Kinship*. Durham, NC: Duke University Press.

Gagnebin, Jeanne Marie. 2005. "Do conceito de mímesis no pensamento de Adorno e Benjamin." In *7ete: Sete Aulas Sobre Linguagem, Memória e História*, 79–104. Rio de Janeiro: Imago.

García, Angela S. 2014. "Hidden in Plain Sight: How Unauthorised Migrants Strategically Assimilate in Restrictive Localities in California." *Journal of Ethnic and Migration Studies* 40 (12): 1895–1914.

Geertz, Clifford. 1973. "Thick Description." In *The Interpretation of Cultures: Selected Essays*, 3–32. New York: Basic Books.

Gefter, Amanda. 2014a. "Complexity on the Horizon." *Nature*, no. 509, 552–53. https://www.nature.com/news/theoretical-physics-complexity-on-the-horizon-1.15285.

——. 2014b. *Trespassing on Einstein's Lawn: A Father, a Daughter, the Meaning of Nothing, and the Beginning of Everything*. New York: Bantam Books.

Gibbs, Anna. 2010. "After Affect: Sympathy, Synchrony, and Mimetic Communication." In *The Affect Theory Reader*, edited by Melissa Gregg and Gregory J. Seigworth, 186–205. Durham, NC: Duke University Press

Gilder, Louisa. 2008. *The Age of Entanglement: When Quantum Physics Was Reborn*. New York: Vintage Books.

Gold, Raymond L. 1958. "Roles in Sociological Field Observations." *Social Forces* 36 (3): 217–23. https://doi.org/10.2307/2573808.

Gomberg-Muñoz, Ruth. 2016. *Becoming Legal: Immigration Law and Mixed Status Families*. New York: Oxford University Press.

Gordon, Avery F. 1997. *Ghostly Matters: Haunting and the Sociological Imagination*. Minneapolis: University of Minnesota Press.

Greene, Brian. 2005. *The Fabric of the Cosmos: Space, Time, and the Texture of Reality*. New York: Vintage.

Greenhouse, Carol J. 1996. *A Moment's Notice: Time Politics across Culture*. Ithaca, NY: Cornell University Press.

Grünewald, Annika. 1980. "Resan tillbaka till Indien" [Journey back to India]. *Att Adoptera* 11 (2): 3–5.

Gupta, Akhil, and James Ferguson, eds. 1997. *Anthropological Locations: Boundaries and Grounds of a Field Science*. Berkeley: University of California Press.

Gusterson, Hugh. 2017. "Homework: Toward a Critical Ethnography of the University." *American Ethnologist* 44 (3): 435–50.

Guzmán, Patricio, dir. 2010. *Nostalgia for the Light*; Brooklyn, NY: Icarus Films, 2011.

Haddon, Alfred C. 1935. *General Ethnography*. Vol. 1 of *Reports of the Cambridge Anthropological Expedition to Torres Straits*. Cambridge: Cambridge University Press.

Hague Convention. 1993. Hague Conference on Private International Law, Final Act of the Seventeenth Session, May 29, 32 I.L.M. 1134. www.hcch.net/index_en.php?act =conventions.text&cid=69.

Hale, Edward Everett. 1900. *The Man without a Country: And Other Stories*. New York City: Little, Brown.

Hamner, Everett L. 2005. "The Gap in the Wall: Partnership, Physics and Politics." In *The New Utopian Politics of Ursula K. Le Guin's "The Dispossessed,"* edited by

Laurence Davis, Peter G. Stillman, et al., 233–46. Lanham, MD: Lexington Books.

Hasselberg, Ines. 2016. *Enduring Uncertainty: Deportation, Punishment and Everyday Life.* New York: Berghahn Books.

Heidegger, Martin. 1962. *Being and Time.* Translated by John Macquarrie and Edward Robinson. Oxford: Basil Blackwell.

——. (1978) 1993. *Basic Writings: Ten Key Essays.* Edited by David Farrell Krell. London: Routledge. Revised and expanded edition, San Francisco, CA: HarperCollins. Citations refer to the HarperCollins edition.

Heller, Nathan. 2021. "What We Get Wrong about Joan Didion." *New Yorker,* January 25, 2021, 1–17. https://www.newyorker.com/magazine/2021/02/01/what-we-get-wrong-about-joan-didion.

Hennessy-Fiske, Molly. 2019. "U.S. Customs Officer Loses Job and Citizenship Case over His Mexican Birth Certificate." *Los Angeles Times,* November 26, 2019. www.latimes.com/world-nation/story/2019-11-26/u-s-customs-officer-loses-job-citizenship-due-to-birth-certificate-challenge.

Hjern, Anders, and Peter Allbeck. 2002. "Suicide in First- and Second-Generation Immigrants in Sweden: A Comparative Study." *Social Psychiatry and Psychiatric Epidemiology,* no. 37, 423–29.

Hjern, Anders, Frank Lindblad, and Bo Vinnerljung. 2002. "Suicide, Psychiatric Illness, and Social Maladjustment in Intercountry Adoptees in Sweden: A Cohort Study." *Lancet,* no. 360, 443–48.

Holslin, Jill Marie. 2020. "Border Hack: Challenging Trump's Spectator Culture." https://drive.google.com/file/d/1SSeMVEP3buaFXFFtX64KoHoFqgli6q1t/view.

Hondagneu-Sotelo, Pierrette, and Ernestine Avila. 1997. "'I'm Here, but I'm There': The Meanings of Latina Transnational Motherhood." *Gender and Society* 11 (5): 548–71.

Horton, Sarah, and Josiah Heyman, eds. 2020. *Paper Trails: Migrants, Documents, and Legal Insecurity.* Durham, NC: Duke University Press.

Hübinette, Tobias. 2004. "Adopted Koreans and the Development of Identity in the 'Third Space.'" *Adoption and Fostering* 28 (1): 16–24. https://doi.org/10.1177/030857590402800104.

——. 2006. "From Orphan Trains to Babylifts: Colonial Trafficking, Empire Building, and Social Engineering." In *Outsiders Within: Writing on Transracial Adoption,* edited by Jane Jeong Trenka, Julia Chinyere Oparah, and Sun Yung Shin, 139–49. Cambridge, MA: South End Press.

Hübinette, Tobias, and Catrin Lundström. 2015. "Three Phases of Hegemonic Whiteness: Understanding Racial Temporalities in Sweden." *Social Identities: Journal for the Study of Race, Nation, and Culture* 20 (6): 123–37. http://dx.doi.org/10.1080/13504630.2015.1004827.

Hull, Matthew S. 2012. "Documents and Bureaucracy." *Annual Review of Anthropology,* no. 41, 251–67.

Husserl, Edmund. 1980. *Phantasie, Bildbewusstsein, Erinnerung.* Edited by Eduard Marbach. The Hague: Martinus Nijhoff.

Iser, Wolfgang. 1993. *The Fictive and the Imaginary: Charting Literary Anthropology.* Baltimore, MD: Johns Hopkins University Press.

Jackson, Jean E. 1990. "'I Am a Fieldnote': Fieldnotes as a Symbol of Professional Identity." In *Fieldnotes: The Makings of Anthropology,* edited by Roger Sanjek, 3–33. Ithaca, NY: Cornell University Press.

Jelin, Elizabeth. 2003. *State Repression and the Labors of Memory.* Minneapolis: University of Minnesota Press.

Johnson, LiLi. 2018. "Searching in Photographs: Photography and the Chinese Birthparent Search." *Adoption and Culture* 6 (1): 115–34.

Jordan, Miriam. 2020. "A Woman without a Country: Adopted at Birth and Deportable at 30." *New York Times*, July 7, 2020. https://www.nytimes.com/2020/07/07/us/immigrants-adoption-ice.html.

Karim, Osmond, dir. 2017. *De ensamma* [The lonely ones]. Swedish Film Institute.

Ketelaar, Eric. 2001. "Tacit Narratives: The Meanings of Archives." *Archival Science* 1 (2): 131–41. https://doi.org/10.1007/BF02435644.

Khosravi, Shahram. 2010. *"Illegal" Traveller: An Auto-Ethnography of Borders*. Basingstoke, UK: Palgrave Macmillan.

Kim, Eleana J. 2010. *Adopted Territory: Transnational Korean Adoptees and the Politics of Belonging*. Durham, NC: Duke University Press.

Klawans, Stuart. 2016. "Review: Fire at Sea." *Film Comment*, September–October 2016. https://www.filmcomment.com/article/review-fire-at-sea-gianfranco-rosi.

Knodt, Eva M. 1995. Foreword to *Social Systems*, by Niklas Luhmann, i–xxxvii. Stanford, CA: Stanford University Press.

Knowlton, Linda Goldstein, dir. 2011. *Somewhere Between*.

Lacan, Jacques. 1977. *Écrits: A Selection*. Translated by A Schneider. New York: W. W. Norton.

Latour, Bruno. 1999. *Pandora's Hope: Essays on the Reality of Science Studies*. Cambridge, MA: Harvard University Press.

Lawrance, Benjamin N., and Jacqueline Stevens, eds. 2017. *Citizenship in Question: Evidentiary Birthright and Statelessness*. Durham, NC: Duke University Press.

Lederman, Rena. 2006. "The Perils of Working at Home: IRB 'Mission Creep' as Context and Content for an Ethnography of Disciplinary Knowledges." *American Ethnologist* 33 (4): 482–91.

Le Guin, Ursula K. 1974. *The Dispossessed*. New York: Avon Books.

——. 1982. "Schrödinger's Cat." In *The Compass Rose*, 41–49. New York: Harper & Row.

——. 2001. *Always Coming Home*. Berkeley: University of California Press.

Liem, Deann Borshay, dir. 2000. *First Person Plural*. Berkeley, CA: Mu Films.

——, dir. 2018. *Geographies of Kinship: The Korean Adoption Story*. Berkeley, CA: Mu Films.

Lindqvist, Bosse, and Bo Ohlén. 2003. *En gång var jag korean* [Once I was Korean]. Aired on Sveriges Television, channel 2.

Llewellyn, Karl N. 1930. "A Realistic Jurisprudence: The Next Step." *Columbia Law Review*, no. 30, 431–65.

Loftus, Elizabeth F. 1993. "The Reality of Repressed Memories." *American Psychologist* 48 (5): 518–37.

López, Jane Lilly. 2021. *Unauthorized Love: Mixed-Citizenship Couples Negotiating Intimacy, Immigration, and the State*. Stanford, CA: Stanford University Press.

Luhmann, Niklas. 1995. *Social Systems*. Translated by John Bednarz Jr. Stanford, CA: Stanford University Press. First published 1984.

Madison, D. Soyini. 2007. "Co-Performative Witnessing." *Cultural Studies* 21 (6): 826–31.

Mahmood, Saba. 2005. *The Politics of Piety: The Islamic Revival and the Feminist Subject*. Princeton, NJ: Princeton University Press.

Marcus, George E., and Michael M. J. Fischer. 1986. *Anthropology as Cultural Critique: An Experimental Moment in the Human Sciences*. 2nd ed. Chicago: University of Chicago Press.

Matar, Hisham. 2016. *The Return: Fathers, Sons and the Land in Between*. New York: Random House.

Mbembe, Achille. 2002. "The Power of the Archive and Its Limits." In *Refiguring the Archive*, edited by Carolyn Hamilton, Verne Harris, Michèle Pickover, Graeme Reid, Razia Saleh, and Jane Taylor, 9–26. Dordrecht: Kluwer Academic.

McDonald, Jeff. 2016. "Former U.S. Rep. Hunter Sued by Family Charging Fraud over Immigration Status of Adopted Kids." *Los Angeles Times*, August 15, 2016. https://www.latimes.com/local/lanow/la-me-duncan-hunter-lawsuit-20160815-snap-story.html.

McFate, Montgomery. 2005. "Anthropology and Counterinsurgency: The Strange Story of Their Curious Relationship." *Military Review*, March–April 2005, 24–38. https://www.hsdl.org/?view&did=452717.

McNally, David. 2006. *Another World Is Possible: Globalization and Anti-capitalism.* Winnipeg, MB: Arbeiter Ring.

Mead, Margaret. 1959. "Introduction." In *An Anthropologist at Work*, by Ruth Benedict, xv–xxii. Cambridge: The Riverside Press.

Menjívar, Cecilia. 2006. "Liminal Legality: Salvadoran and Guatemalan Immigrants' Lives in the United States." *American Journal of Sociology* 111 (4): 999–1037.

Mermin, N. David. 1990. "Extreme Quantum Entanglement in a Superposition of Macroscopically Distinct States." *Physical Review Letters* 65 (15): 1838–40.

Milner, Marion. 1969. *The Hands of the Living God*. London: Hogarth Press and the Institute of Psycho-Analysis.

Mitchell, Julie, and Susan Bibler Coutin. 2019. "Living Documents in Transnational Spaces of Migration between El Salvador and the United States." *Law and Social Inquiry* 44 (4): 865–92.

Modell, Judith S. 1994. *Kinship with Strangers: Adoption, and Interpretations of Kinship in American Culture.* Berkeley: University of California Press.

Montoya, Margaret. 1994. "Mascaras, Trenzas, y Greñas: Un/Masking the Self While Un/Braiding Latina Stories and Legal Discourse." *Harvard Journal of Law and Gender*, no. 17, 185–220.

Morrissey, Kate. 2017. "Border Wall Prototypes Become Canvas for Light Graffiti." *Los Angeles Times*, November 22, 2017. https://www.latimes.com/local/lanow/la-me-border-wall-project-20171122-story.html.

Mountz, Alison, Richard Wright, Ines Miyares, and Adrian J. Bailey. 2002. "Lives in Limbo: Temporary Protected Status and Immigrant Identities." *Global Networks* 2 (4): 335–56. https://doi.org/10.1111/1471-0374.00044.

Ms. L. v. US Immigration and Customs Enforcement, Order Granting Plaintiffs' Motion for Classwide Preliminary Injunction. https://s3.documentcloud.org/documents/4561268/SDCA-L-v-ICE-injunction.pdf

Muñiz, Ana. 2019. "Bordering Circuitry: Crossjurisdictional Immigration Surveillance." *UCLA Law Review*, no. 66, 1636–82.

Nadeau, Robert, and Menas Kafatos. 1999. *The Non-local Universe: The New Physics and Matters of the Mind.* Oxford: Oxford University Press.

Nader, Laura. 1972. "Up the Anthropologist: Perspectives Gained from Studying Up." In *Reinventing Anthropology*, edited by Dell Hymes, 284–311. New York: Vintage Books.

Nancy, Jean-Luc. 1993. "Abandoned Being." In *The Birth to Presence*, edited by Jean-Luc Nancy, 36–47. Trans. by Brian Holmes & others. Stanford: Stanford University Press.

Nelsen Aaron. 2021. "'I Just Needed to Find My Family': The Scandal of Chile's Stolen Children." *Guardian*, January 26, 2021. https://www.theguardian.com/news/2021/jan/26/chile-stolen-children-international-adoption-sweden.

Ngai, Mae M. 2004. *Impossible Subjects: Illegal Aliens and the Making of Modern America.* Princeton, NJ: Princeton University Press.

Nietzsche, Friedrich 1977. *Morgenröte* (Werke, I), 8th ed., edited and published by Karl Schlechta. Munich.

Nordin, Sara. 1996. "Mer eller mindre svart" [More or less Black]. *SvartVitt*, no. 1, 4–6.

Ombres, Frank. 2014. "Open Roads Interview: Gianfranco Rosi." *Film Comment*, June 6, 2014. https://www.filmcomment.com/blog/interview-gianfranco-rosi.

Ordoñez, Juan Thomas. 2016. "Documents and Shifting Labor Environments among Undocumented Migrant Workers in Northern California." *Anthropology of Work Review* 37 (1): 24–33.

Pais, Abraham. 1991. *Niels Bohr's Times in Physics, Philosophy, and Polity*. Oxford: Oxford University Press.

Passaro, Joanne. 1997. "You Can't Take the Subway to the Field: Village Epistemologies in the Global Village." In *Anthropological Locations: Boundaries and Grounds of a Field Science*, edited by Akhil Gupta and Jams Ferguson, 147–62. Berkeley: University of California Press.

Phillips, Adam. 1988. *Winnicott*. Cambridge, MA: Harvard University Press.

Posocco, Silvia. 2011. "Expedientes: Fissured Legality and Affective States in the Transnational Adoption Archives in Guatemala." *Law, Culture and the Humanities* 7 (3): 434–56.

Prébin, Elise. 2013. *Meeting Once More: The Korean Side of Transnational Adoption*. New York: New York University Press.

Probyn, Elspeth. 1996. *Outside Belongings*. New York: Routledge.

Rapp, Rayna, and Faye Ginsburg. 2011. "Reverberations: Disability and the New Kinship Imaginary." *Anthropological Quarterly* 84 (2): 379–410.

Ricoeur, Paul. 1991. "Life in Quest of Narrative." In *On Paul Ricoeur: Narrative and Interpretation*, edited by David Wood, 20–33. London: Routledge.

Riles, Annelise. 2006. "Anthropology, Human Rights, and Legal Knowledge: Culture in the Iron Cage." *American Anthropologist* 108 (1): 52–65.

——. 2011. *Collateral Knowledge: Legal Reasoning in the Global Financial Markets*. Chicago: University of Chicago Press.

Rony, Fatimah Tobing. 1996. *The Third Eye: Race, Cinema, and Ethnographic Spectacle*. Durham, NC: Duke University Press Books.

Rose, Jacqueline. 1996. *States of Fantasy*. Oxford: Clarendon Press.

Rosi, Gianfranco, dir. 2016. *Fire at Sea*. Rai: Italy.

Rovelli, Carlo. 1996. "Relational Quantum Mechanics." *International Journal of Theoretical Physics*, no. 35, 1637–78.

——. 2021. *Helgoland: Making Sense of the Quantum Revolution*. Translated by Erica Segre and Simon Carnell. New York: Riverhead Books.

Said, Edward. 1979. *Orientalism*. New York: Vintage Books.

Sammarco, Lovisa. 2003. "The Bright Star—en kulturbrygga" [The Bright Star—a cultural bridge]. *NIA Informerar*, no. 2, 6–7.

Sanchez, Linda E. 2020. "Facing COVID-19 as an Undocumented Essential Worker." *Sapiens*, December 3, 2020. https://www.sapiens.org/culture/covid-undocumented-essential-workers.

Sandhu, Sukhdev. 2012. "Patricio Guzmán, Chile's Master of Documentary, Focuses on the Stars." *Guardian*, July 20, 2012. http://www.theguardian.com/film/2012/jul/20/patricio-guzman-chile-master-documentary.

Schindele, Anna ChuChu. 2022. "Adopting a position—analyzing, theorizing and decolonizing transnational and transracial adoption in Sweden." *The British Journal of Social Work*, bcac083, https://doi.org/10.1093/bjsw/bcac083, published 13 May 2022.

Schneider, David M. 1980. *American Kinship: A Cultural Account.* Chicago: University of Chicago Press.

Schrödinger, Erwin. 1935. "Die gegenwärtige Situation in der Quantenmechanik" [The present situation in quantum mechanics]. *Naturwissenschaften* 23 (48): 807–12.

Schwab, Gabriele. 2010. *Haunting Legacies: Violent Histories and Transgenerational Trauma.* New York: Columbia University Press.

Seif, Kevin. 2018. "U.S. Is Denying Passports to Americans along the Border, Throwing Their Citizenship into Question." *Washington Post,* September 13, 2018. https:// www.washingtonpost.com/world/the_americas/us-is-denying-passports-to -americans-along-the-border-throwing-their-citizenship-into-question/2018/08 /29/1d630e84-a0da-11e8-a3dd-2a1991f075d5_story.html.

Sekkel, Marie Claire. 2016. "The Play and the Invention of the World in Walter Benjamin and Donald Winnicott." *Psicologia USP* 27 (1): 86–95. https://doi.org/10.1590 /0103-656420140016.

Simmel, Georg. 1990. *Philosophy of Money.* Translated by Tom Bottomore and D. Frisby. New York: Routledge.

Sjöblom, Lisa Wool-Rim. 2019. *Palimpsest: Documents from a Korean Adoption.* Montreal: Drawn & Quarterly.

Smith, Linda Tuhiwai. 2012. *Decolonizing Methodologies: Research and Indigenous Peoples.* 2nd ed. London: Zed Books. First published 1999.

Spencer-Brown, George. 1972. *Laws of Form.* New York: Julian Press. First published 1969.

Steedman, Carolyn. 2009. "'Something She Called a Fever': Michelet, Derrida, and Dust (Or, in the Archives with Michelet and Derrida)." In *Archives, Documentation and Institutions of Social Memory: Essays from the Sawyer Seminar,* edited by Francis X. Blouin Jr. and William G. Rosenberg, 4–19. Ann Arbor: University of Michigan Press.

Stern, Daniel N. 1985. *The Interpersonal World of the Infant: A View from Psychoanalysis and Developmental Psychology.* New York: Basic Books.

Stern, Daniel N. 2004. *The Present Moment in Psychotherapy and Everyday Life.* New York: W. W. Norton.

Stjerna, Ingrid. 1976. "Biologiska mamman—ett hot?" [The biological mother—a threat?]. *Att Adoptera* 7 (3): 100–101.

——. 2004. *The Present Moment in Psychotherapy and Everyday Life.* New York: W. W. Norton.

Stoler, Ann Laura. 2010. *Along the Archival Grain: Epistemic Anxieties and Colonial Common Sense.* Princeton, NJ: Princeton University Press.

Stone-Cadena, Victoria, and Soledad Álvarez Velasco. 2018. "Historicizing Mobility: *Coyoterismo* in the Indigenous Ecuadorian Migration Industry." *Annals of the American Academy of Political and Social Science* 676 (1): 194–211.

Strathern, Marilyn. 1999. "The Ethnographic Effect I." In *Property, Substance and Effect: Anthropological Essays on Persons and Things,* 1–28. London: Athlone Press.

——. 2005. *Kinship, Law and the Unexpected: Relatives Are Always a Surprise.* Cambridge: Cambridge University Press.

Susskind, Leonard. 2016. "Computational Complexity and Black Hole Horizons." *Fortschritte der physik* [Progress of physics] 64 (1): 24–43. Article first appeared in preprint form in 2014; available at http://arxiv.org/abs/1402.5674v2.

Talu, Yonca. 2016. "Interview: Gianfranco Rosi." *Film Comment,* October 24, 2016. https://www.filmcomment.com/blog/interview-gianfranco-rosi-fire-at-sea.

Thomas, Deborah A. 2016. "Time and the Otherwise: Plantations, Garrisons and Being Human in the Caribbean." *Anthropological Theory* 16 (2–3): 177–200.

Tranströmer, Tomas. 1997. "Answers to Letters." In *New Collected Poems*, translated by Robert Fulton, 136–37. Newcastle upon Tyne: Bloodaxe Books.

Trenka, Jane Jeong. 2003. *The Language of Blood*. Minneapolis: Borealis Books.

——. 2009. *Fugitive Visions: An Adoptee's Return to Korea*. Minneapolis: Graywolf Press.

Trotzig, Astrid. 1996. *Blod Är Tjockare Än Vatten* [Blood is thicker than water]. Stockholm: Albert Bonniers Förlag.

United Nations General Assembly. 1989. Resolution 44/25, Convention on the Rights of the Child. November 20, 1989. https://www.un.org/en/development/desa/popul ation/migration/generalassembly/docs/globalcompact/A_RES_44_25.pdf.

United States Citizenship and Immigration Services. N.d. "Green Card for Immigrant Investors." Accessed December 29, 2021. https://www.uscis.gov/greencard/investors.

United States District Court, Southern District of California. 2018. "Order Granting Plaintiffs' Motion for Classwide Preliminary Injunction," *Ms. L v. ICE*, June 26, 2018. https://assets.documentcloud.org/documents/4561268/SDCA-L-v-ICE-injunc tion.pdf.

Vaihinger, Hans. 1922. *Die Philosophie des Als Ob. System der theroetischen, praktischen und religiösen Fiktionen der Menschheit auf Grund eines idealistischen Positivismus*. 8th ed. Leipzig: Verlag von Felix Meiner.

——. 1952. *The Philosophy of "As If": A System of the Theoretical, Practical and Religious Fictions of Mankind*. Translated by C. K. Ogden. London: Routledge and Kegan Paul.

Van Raamsdonk, Mark. 2010. "Building Up Spacetime with Quantum Entanglement." *General Relativity and Gravitation*, no. 42, 2323–29.

Vismann, Cornelia. 2008. *Files: Law and Media Technology*. Translated by Geoffrey Winthrop-Young. Stanford, CA: Stanford University Press.

Visweswaran, Kamala. 1994. *Fictions of Feminist Ethnography*. Minneapolis: University of Minnesota Press.

Von Melen, Anna. 1998. *Samtal med vuxna adopterade* [Conversations with adult adoptees]. Stockholm: Rabén Prisma.

Wagner, Roy. 1981. *The Invention of Culture*. Rev. ed. Chicago: University of Chicago Press. First published 1975.

Waldron, Jan L. 1995. *Giving Away Simone*. New York: Random House.

Walker, Eric. 2018. "Mourning, Adoption, and Literary Form." *Adoption and Culture* 6 (1): 11–14.

Wallensteen, Hanna. 2000. *Veta sin plats* [Know your place]. Monologue in one act. Private collection of Barbara Yngvesson.

——. 2021. "Psykologen om rasism och minoritetsstress—och uppväxten som adopterad" [The psychologist on racism and minority stress—and growing up as an adoptee]. Invited talk for *Sommar och Vinter i P1*, Sveriges Radio, July 19, 2021. https:// sverigesradio.se/avsnitt/hanna-wallensteen-sommarprat-se.

Watson, Steven. 2020. "George Spencer-Brown's Laws of Form Fifty Years on: Why We Should Be Giving More Attention in Mathematics Education." In Special issue on Philosophy of Mathematics Education, *Mathematics Teaching Research Journal* 12 (2): 161–87.

Weber, Max. 1968. *Economy and Society: An Outline of Interpretive Sociology*. Edited by Guenther Roth and Claus Wittich. New York: Bedminster Press.

Weld, Kirsten. 2014. *Paper Cadavers: The Archives of Dictatorship in Guatemala*. Durham, NC: Duke University Press.

Wheeler, John Archibald. 1994. "Time Today." In *Physical Origins of Time Asymmetry*, edited by J. J. Halliwell, J. Pérez-Mercader, and W. H. Zurek. Cambridge: Cambridge University Press.

——. 1996. *At Home in the Universe*. Melville NY: AIP Press.

Williams, Patricia J. 1991. *The Alchemy of Race and Rights*. Cambridge, MA: Harvard University Press, 1991.

Winkvist, Hanna Markusson. 2006. "Defining a New Family: The Swedish Approach to Intercountry Adoption." Paper presented at Sixth European Social Science History Conference, Amsterdam, March 22–25.

Winnicott, D. W. 1971. *Playing and Reality*. London: Tavistock.

Woods, Wind. 2015. *The Service Workers Project: Against the Current/Contra la Corriente*. Play performed by the Brown Bag Theatre Company, UC Irvine, May 2015. http://howlround.com/livestreaming-performance-of-the-service-workers-project-contra-la-corrienteagainst-the-current.

Wright, Eric. 2008. "Gregory Bateson: Epistemology, Language, Play and the Double Bind." *Anthropoetics* 14 (1). http://anthropoetics.ucla.edu/ap1401/1401wright.

Wright, Michelle. 2015. *Physics of Blackness: Beyond the Middle Passage Epistemology*. Minneapolis: University of Minnesota Press.

Yngvesson, Barbara. 1997. "Negotiating Motherhood: Identity and Difference in 'Open' Adoptions." *Law and Society Review* 31 (1): 31–80.

——. 2000. "'Un Niño de Cualquier Color': Race and Nation in Intercountry Adoption." In *Globalizing Institutions: Case Studies in Regulation and Innovation*, edited by Jane Jenson and Boaventura de Sousa Santos, 169–204. Ashcroft, UK: Ashgate.

——. 2002. "Placing the 'Gift Child' in Transnational Adoption." *Law and Society Review* 36 (2): 227–56.

——. 2005. "Going 'Home': Adoption, Loss of Bearings, and the Mythology of Roots." In *Cultures of Transnational Adoption*, edited by Toby Alice Volkman, 25–48. Durham, NC: Duke University Press.

——. 2010. *Belonging in an Adopted World: Race, Identity, and Transnational Adoption*. Chicago: University of Chicago Press.

——. 2013. "The Child Who Was Left Behind: 'Dynamic Temporality' and Interpretations of History in Transnational Adoption." *Childhood* 20 (3): 354–67.

Yngvesson, Barbara, and Susan Bibler Coutin. 2006. "Backed by Papers: Undoing Persons, Histories, and Return." *American Ethnologist* 33 (2): 177–90. https://doi.org/10.1525/ae.2006.33.2.177.

——. 2008. "Schrödinger's Cat and the Ethnography of Law." *PoLAR: Political and Legal Anthropology Review* 31 (1): 61–78.

Yoshimi, Shunya. 2006. "Information." *Theory, Culture, and Society* 23 (2–3): 271–88.

Zavella, Patricia. 2011. *I'm Neither Here nor There: Mexicans' Quotidian Struggles with Migration and Poverty*. Durham, NC: Duke University Press.

Žižek, Slavoj. 1989. *The Sublime Object of Ideology*. London: Verso.

Zuberi, Tukufu, and Eduardo Bonilla-Silva, E., eds. 2008. *White Logic, White Methods: Racism and Methodology*. Lanham, MD: Rowman and Littlefield.

Index

www.ingramcontent.com/pod-product-compliance
Lightning Source LLC
Chambersburg PA
CBHW032353280326
41935CB00008B/554